MARCEL SCHNEIDER

Translated by Elizabeth Poston

Schubert

GREENWOOD PRESS, PUBLISHERS
WESTPORT, CONNECTICUT

Library of Congress Cataloging in Publication Data

Schneider, Marcel, 1913-
Schubert.

Reprint of the ed. published by Grove Press, New York, which was issued as no. 4 of Evergreen profile books.
Bibliography: p.
Discography: p.
1. Schubert, Franz Peter, 1797-1828.
[ML410.S2922 1975] 780'.92'4 [B] 75-28926
ISBN 0-8371-8472-X

(E. T. A. Hoffmann.)

This edition originally published in 1959 by Grove Press Inc., New York

Reprinted with the permission of Grove Press, Inc.

Reprinted in 1975 by Greenwood Press, a division of Williamhouse-Regency Inc.

Library of Congress Catalog Card Number 75-28926

ISBN 0-8371-8472-X

Printed in the United States of America

Schubert
by Marcel Schneider

Contents

Heaven

When Stravinsky was asked if he was not sent to sleep by the prolixities of Schubert, he replied:

'What does it matter if, when I awake, it seems to me that I am in paradise?'

Schubert's music evokes heaven – or rather, expresses the longing for it. But what heaven? Not, certainly, the heaven of the theologians, nor yet that of Dante, but a heavenly state of innocence, candour, tenderness, the place where those meet together who loved each other well on earth. Schubert's music is an aspiration towards this lost paradise. In this lies its power to move us and hold us spellbound, it is in this sense that it is like no other music, communicating with us in a language all its own.

Although Schubert lived a life that, with its share of frailty and indulgence, was no worse than that of other men, it seems as though in heaven he had a new sign of the zodiac, for was he not vowed to the world of the spirit by his patron saint, Franz Seraph, Blessed Francis of Assisi?

A favourite painting by Giovanni di Paolo that hangs in the Academy of Fine Arts in Siena, would surely have appealed to Franz Seraph if he had ever been to Italy: he would have

Franz Schubert.

The Last Judgment by Giovanni di Paolo (Siena.)

seen depicted in it the heaven of his dreams. In an orchard of trees bearing both fruit and blossom, beneath which small hares frolic among plants of strawberry, burnet and thyme, the blessed souls who loved on earth stretch out their arms to one another in embrace, and set forth into eternity two by two ... husband and wife, lover and lover, mother and child, monks, nuns, a bishop and his page, old men, young girls in the Isles of the Blest beside the waters of comfort, where our laws and prejudices are of no account. Untrammelled by their bodies,

chosen of each other, these souls achieve the perfect freedom of love; theirs is the joy of identification within a single entity, of being able to say: 'I am thyself.'

The heaven of Schubert's imagination was a garden of eternal youth, a place where there was always music, where happiness is the wellspring of spontaneous, overflowing delight: a divine vision more of feeling than dogma, with the precedence allowed to love over faith; an admission that it is the passion of love that gives life its meaning, beauty and

joy. In that other world of Schubert's it is the heart that prevails.

It is not hard to imagine Schubert's choice of companions for his paradise garden: his dearest affections were for his family, his lively, normal friendships, and the tender amours of love. He was above all responsive to goodness. In 1822, in a remarkable fragment of autobiography which he calls *My dream*, he says of his parents: *They were good. I was bound to them by deep devotion.* And of Theresa Grob, the sweetheart of his youth, he says: *She was good, wholeheartedly good.*

His brief span of scarcely thirty-two years is offset by a long aftermath in which he is seen by succeeding generations as forever surrounded by those he loved: his gentle, self-effacing mother, his father who so efficiently supervised his musical education, his brothers Ignaz and Ferdinand, and his friends Schober, Hüttenbrenner, Spaun, Mayrhofer, Moritz von Schwind, Kupelwieser, his beloveds, Theresa and Caroline – the circle who were the loves of his life.

In his life, distinguished by nothing fantastic or extraordinary, the psalmist's words were to be fulfilled: *Man hath but a short time to live*, so that it is scarcely possible to think of his birth without his death – a lasting impression left by the experience of listening to a performance given in his birthplace of his *String Quartet in D minor* (*Death and the Maiden*).

He was born on 31 January 1797 in the Viennese suburb of Lichtenthal, where his father was master in charge of the parish school. The schoolmaster's lodgings at the sign of 'The Red Crayfish' (Zum Rothen Krebs) in the street that is now the Nussdorferstrasse, were on a site formerly the property of the monastery of Am Himmelpfortgrund (The Gate of Paradise) – heaven again! It seemed as if Schubert could not escape it.

The house is typical of other such homely Central European houses, with an unpretentious exterior, an inner courtyard with shrubs and evergreens, an iron balcony along the length of the first floor and a glass verandah above the main gateway, a couple of wings with lofty roofs, and a garden with maple trees looking on to the Jesuit-style twin towers of the church of the Twelve Apostles. Four years later, in 1801, the Schubert family had saved enough to be able to buy a home of their own at the sign of 'The Black Horse'.

Franz Schubert the elder, who was of Moravian peasant

Birthplace of Franz Schubert.

stock, had settled in Vienna in 1784, and married there the daughter of a Silesian locksmith, Elisabeth Vitz, who bore him fourteen children of whom only five survived to maturity – a humble home that was to give to the world the most characteristically Viennese of Vienna's composers. Schubert, like Beethoven, was the son of a domestic servant, but unlike Strindberg, he did not have the sad experience of early suffering: the deep humility and sunny sweetness of Schubert's nature helped to spare him that misery. Born in Vienna, spending most of his life there and dying there, he was content to know himself the embodiment of Austrian music,

Schubert's parents

the destined genius of the *lied.* He did not bother about worldly honours.

The home was not poor or sordid: Schubert's childhood was a happy one, full of music. But although the occasion of the open air performance of his music in the courtyard of his early home provided a peaceful opportunity to ponder upon his childhood, it was not of the happy child one thought as one heard the opening bars of the *D minor Quartet* (*Death and the Maiden*), but the exhausted man dying at thirty-two.

For although the first movement is filled with a sense of past joys, the gaiety of childhood, all of youth's trust and radiance since its beginnings, it affirms no less Schubert's challenge to death. Death is present, watching the composer as he watches also the young girl of Claudius's poem. How will Schubert meet what has there been revealed to him: will he, we wonder, cry out in anguish, hurl defiance at heaven, or will he accept his destiny and go with hand outstretched to meet what is to come?

After the defiant tumult of the first movement, the variations of the second, in which is heard the grave, serene, insinuating voice of death, bring a sense of resignation to the inevitable. Schubert's premature death seems even more pathetic in the surroundings of his carefree childhood, and with the deliberate monotony of the rhythm and the music's insistence, the thought becomes impelling that his precocious and prolific genius was endemic in the appointed brevity of his life, and that it was not by an ordinary stroke of chance that he died.

Schubert sees death not as a biblical manifestation of God's wrath, deserved of our sins, but death who becomes friend, confidant and comforter, the figure opening to us the translucent portals of the world beyond. Its symbol is no longer the grinning skeleton of our medieval Dance of Death; Schubert's conception is nearer to the Eleusinian mysteries of ancient Greece:

> Give me your hand, lovely and tender child!
> I am your friend, I come not to chasten.
> Be of good cheer! I am not to be feared,
> You will sleep sweetly in my arms!

The figure of Death who murmurs into the Maiden's ear these comforting words is twin brother of Sleep whom the Greeks portrayed as a beautiful boy bearing a dipped torch.

The Scherzo returns to the force of the opening, with an indescribably frantic quality in the rhythm, which Wagner uses in *Siegfried*, when the young hero forges his sword, and with which Schubert prepares us for the terrifying dance of death of the final Presto. Schubert accepts his death, he takes it to himself, abandoning himself with it to a wild dance of mingled delirium and despair, laughter and tears – the marriage of heaven and hell. In his death is also his source of life: his compelling, enigmatical genius allows him no peace. He must compose, unrecognised by the world, scorned by it, until he is worn out – but what of it? In Goethe's words, quoting Socrates, Schubert's genius, his 'demon' made of him a visionary, transporting him, consuming and transfiguring him.

The music's impetus is interspersed with short, quieter passages that appear as glimpses of the past, backward glances toward all that is gone for ever, that Schubert knows he can never recapture – peace of heart, faith in the future, idyllic childhood; and he whirls ever faster in the dance as he clasps to him his genius and his death, the two now become one.

But if Schubert's music is heavenly, he was far from being particularly devout. At college he never received more than mediocre marks for religious instruction. Throughout his life he had a simple faith compounded more of religious sentiment than mystical fervour; he was religious in a romantic way, rather than in the stricter sense of the term. He believed in inviolable right to opinion, a belief which included also nature, in an unformulated apprehension of Providence. Brought up in the Catholic faith, he was to remain deeply rooted in the Church, untroubled by Pascal's gnawing doubts. He did not ask himself whether God existed: for him the question simply did not arise, since music is the most intangible of all the arts, the one that restores us to our first innocence, the Ariadne's thread that is our link with our lost paradise; and making music is the supreme way of glorifying God.

Jean-Paul, the great contemporary who inspired Schumann with his romantic philosophy, though there is no evidence that he was read by Schubert, composed an Invocation to Music that sums up Schubert's work:

'O Music, echo of another world, manifestation of a divine being within ourselves, when speech is impotent and our hearts are numb, yours alone is the voice with which men cry out to one another from the depths of their prison, you it is who end their desolation, in whom are resolved the lonely outpourings of their grief.'

There we have it all: music's source in the divine, its preternatural power, its capacity to comfort and to drive away evil, above all, its chief grace of dispelling loneliness, the burden common to mankind, yet natural to none. For music is above all communion.

It is a mystery; and because it is non-representational, intangible, without precise significance, it pertains, to us, to the supernatural, beyond apprehension. Although, of its nature, it must conform to the discipline of the strictest rules, we find in it the purest form of creative inspiration, a total liberation within its power and wonder. It is indeed an echo of another world.

Schubert could not conceive of music in any other way. While still a child, he writes of Mozart's *G minor Symphony: It disturbs me without my knowing why. Its Minuet is enchanting, and it seems to me that in the Trio one can hear angels singing with the orchestra.*

It certainly seemed that he was at home with the heavenly host. To his earliest teachers his youthful mastery seemed little short of miraculous. His father taught him the violin, his brother Ignaz the piano, Michael Holzer, the choirmaster

A Musician's Dream, by Caspar David Friedrich.

of the parish church, singing, organ and thorough-bass. After only a few lessons, it was Schubert who taught his teachers. 'When I thought to teach him something new', notes his father, 'Franz knew it already.' And a few years later, Ruczinska, his professor at college, exclaimed: 'I have nothing more to teach him, he has been taught by God.'

It is certainly tempting to see a divine source in an utterance as amazing as music, particularly when it achieves a maturity of expression far in advance of the artist's intellectual maturity. Schubert, like Mozart, is astonishing for the quality of his work as much as for his youth when it reached such a degree of authority – and he died at an age when Beethoven was only beginning to find an individual style. He wrote his *First Symphony* at the age of sixteen, and in the following year, on 19 October 1814, his song *Gretchen am Spinnrade*. The next year, his most prolific in compositions of all sorts, followed that masterpiece among songs, *Erlkönig*. Such fertility and variety, such grace and such emotional power are surely the signs of a prodigy of genius, inviting assessment on the very highest plane. We attribute to genius that which is beyond our comprehension, although Valéry declares: 'Genius is logic, it is never a mystery... Genius is easy. I mean simply that I know how it works.' The last word may be left to Beethoven: 'In Schubert there is truly divine fire.'

Those who know Schubert only by his legend – a legend perpetuated today in films, operettas and fiction biographies – see him as an artless sentimentalist, simple and rather limited, a sort of Parsifal of song, an angelic simpleton who produced his melodies as a tree bears fruit. Without doubt, Schubert possessed in full measure the virtue of humility; he sought neither worldly honour nor acclamation, and held the love of family and the precious joys of home above all materialism. He was always ready to efface himself, and would go to the piano so that others might dance – an action very characteristic of him in daily life.

But inasmuch as he was an artist, he was well aware of his talent and very proud of his powers. He refused part-time teaching, preferring to give all his time to composition. The uncertainties of artistic life did not weigh upon him because he endured all for music. He had a lofty conception of art, of the creator and his vocation, a mystery which he reverenced first of all in himself. He felt his whole duty to be the writing

Schubert at the piano, by Kupelwieser.

of music, and in his view it would have been fitting that he should be awarded a State pension to save him material worry; for though he was humble, Schubert knew his own value. We are reminded of Saint François de Sales, when he lived at the impressive mansion of Favre at Annecy, sleeping humbly amidst the fleshpots, in order, so he said, that after he had moved among the mighty all day as a bishop, he should remember that he was just an ordinary man, and retire to sleep as François de Sales. With Schubert it was likewise, but in reverse: he passed unnoticed in the world, but when he sat down at his work table, he became Godlike. We cannot doubt it when we hear *An die Musik:* all that music meant for him is expressed in that song. He said one day: *I am in the world only for the purpose of composing* – and today, we cannot doubt it.

One of the characters in Thomas Mann's novel *The Magic*

Mountain, the Italian, Settembrini, considers music from Bach to Wagner to be the supremely German art. He speaks of it as being contrary to progress and the spirit's medium, and proceeds to give an unsympathetic account of it, in which he includes Germanic and Latin literary cultures. 'Music', he says, 'is vague, ambiguous, irresponsive, sterile. You may argue that it is capable of logic: well, spring water can be clear, and if music is clear, where does that get us? It is not something that has true clarity, true logic, but only a dreamlike logic of a world of fantasy that is without meaning and leaves us uncommitted... And even allowing for a more liberal attitude towards music, well and good: music appeals to your feelings, when what matters is the appeal to reason. Music seems to be movement itself.'

If we revert to this definition, without its more derogatory implications, it may fittingly be applied to the music of Schubert, which is indeed movement itself. Moreover, this quality of dynamism in Schubert is tempered with grave lyricism and an intensity of tenderness – an indefinable longing at once desire and regret, an appeal to a realm that he sees as our primordial heritage, to hope in providence, in a dispensation that may yet change the world. Man travels ever onwards towards a destination that dissolves and vanishes before him, his way lies, in the traditional words, through this valley of tears. Schubert saw himself as a traveller, a wayfarer. Many of his scores appear in the guise of charts of his way, or rather, of digressions into the shadows, in face of the immanent destination of death, the far-off bourne of the unattainable heaven that had haunted him since childhood. His two most famous song cycles, *Die Schöne Müllerin* and *Die Winterreise*, are quests of desperation, so is the *Wanderer Fantasy*, and it may be said that his symphonies are founded in the rhythm of footfall. One of his commentators has written: 'Since the advent of sonata form with two main subjects and their closely-knit elaboration that culminated in the Development Section of Beethoven, it has been customary to interpret the great crux of music as tension, contest. In Schubert's symphonies there is neither deliberate tension nor – in the orthodox sense – development; we discern man's footfall, his heartbeat, the eternal wanderer in search of his homeland.'

Ultimately, the dynamics of music can only spring from the continual flux of man's inner life, the interplay of the emotions, the onward surging impulse, the restlessness, longing, regret, joy and sorrow that sweep us along in our search for a lost treasure, the quest of a blissful haven of peace and delight. The sustained aspiration in Schubert's music points us heavenward, to a heaven both desired and possessed. His works appear as fragments of an unfinished tone-poem that never loses itself in introspection, and is neither final achievement nor yet meditation, but movement, action, poetry. To those with the predilection for musicology and obsession with form, Schubert's greatness will remain unapprehended: it is his passionate affirmation of a world beyond, that is the unique factor in his lyrical genius.

Earth

So much for heaven. But there is a body to be reckoned with, and Franz was a Seraph in grotesque garb.

While he was still young, it passed muster. With his wiry hair, thick lips and flattened nose, he had the appearance of a white Negro. A drawing of him at the age of seventeen by Schober shows an appealing profile: one can quite imagine that he attracted his young neighbour, Theresa Grob, with the innocence of first love – according to La Bruyère, the only true love, for that which comes after is less instinctive. Schubert was so short of stature that he was counted unfit for military service, and with indifferent health, his sole assets as a suitor would seem to have been a wistful expression, his handsome brown curls and flashing teeth, an effect describable as a slightly wicked charm.

But it all disappeared very quickly. Too much food and excess of drink, a lack of personal fastidiousness, no capacity for the subtleties of philandering, and a measure of depravity gave him the squat, pot-bellied figure and puffy features perpetuated by legend – and this without account of the spectacles which, it was said, he did not take off even for sleeping, whether this was so that he might be ready to note down a theme from the

Crayon drawing by Moritz von Schwind.

moment of his awakening, or as a palliative in the particular misery of the myopic, who live in a world rendered perilous in its blurred and wavering contours.

At the café he enveloped himself in clouds of smoke, as he did during his morning working hours, and he took no trouble with his appearance. It was by pure chance that the poet Hoffmann von Fallensleben, on a visit to Vienna, happened to see Schubert properly dressed.

He had certainly nothing of the angelic about him, nothing of the elegant courtier of Mozart, nor even, of a conventional man-about-town. In the last three years of his life, when he had acquired the nickname of "Schwammerl" it seems as though he had lost all hope of making himself attractive to women.

The watercolour portrait by Wilhelm August Rieder (1825) is considered to be his best likeness; in it we see him as a reasonably plain man, still radiating vitality. The crayon drawing by Moritz von Schwind shows him already bloated, aged and careworn. A romantic and rather flattering portrait in oils dating from 1827, probably by Mähler, shows him as emaciated and unhappy. Doubtless it would be better to imagine him according to his music, a soul-portrait that would be truer than the most realistic likeness – the body, alas, too often fails to conform with the spirit it harbours.

In the last two years of his life, Schubert triumphed over his nerves and loneliness, and finally accepted the inevitability of pain, his own decline, and, we may suspect, the prospect of his approaching death. The certainty that he had been a true artist and written good music must have consoled him for what he had not attained; but his self-reliance and trust in God were achieved at the cost of anguish and tears – the toll exacted of those who die undefeated.

The hazards of love are precious if illusory: Schubert was not happy in love. The love of his youth was Theresa Grob. She lived in Lichtenthal, had a pretty soprano voice, and though not a beauty, was charming, gentle and good.

On Sunday 16 October 1814 Schubert's *First Mass in F*, for vocal quartet, organ and orchestra was performed in the Lichtenthal church. Schubert conducted, Theresa sang the soprano solo. He was seventeen, she, fourteen; it seems puzzling that they should not have been happy, particularly as the work

Watercolour by W. A. Rieder.

Lichtenthal Church: the interior (F. Kopallik).

was well received and was given again ten days later in the Augustine church in Vienna. Herr Schubert, senior, full of enthusiasm, gave his son a piano, but Schubert, at the time, was earning 40 fl. a year as his father's assistant Herr Grob was looking for a wealthier suitor, and he did not offer Schubert his daughter's hand. Hüttenbrenner tells us that in 1821, after the breach, Schubert confided freely to him his story as the poor young suitor, and his wooing of the gentle sweetheart who bowed to parental authority. *For three years I hoped to marry her, but I could find no situation that would meet our needs. So she married another man, because her parents wished it. I still love her, and since then no other can please me so well or better. The fact is, she was not destined for me.*

She was not destined to marry Schubert, for in 1820 she married a rich miller whom she did not love. The miller's wife, runs the song, has wealth that cost her nothing: but for Theresa, the cost was high.

Schubert, however, consoled himself. Habitually reticent, he was frank about Theresa because he looked on her as his betrothed; he suppressed the name of his second love because he had no hope. His biographers have been at pains to find out the truth. It is known that he made two visits to Count Johann Esterhazy at the Castle of Zelesz. During his second visit in 1824, Schubert became attracted to the younger daughter, then aged seventeen, a suit for which there might have been some hope. Caroline, whose pet-name in the family circle was Cardine, had a sweet and good disposition, though no more pretensions to beauty than Theresa. Whether the two vowed a spiritual union, a relationship of mystical marriage, is not known; the fact is that Caroline did not marry until twenty years later, and that her marriage was declared null when she died at the age of forty-six. Schubert, who was not of the estate to marry an Esterhazy, would not by then have asked Caroline's hand if he had been of royal blood, for by 1824, he knew himself to be infected.

He had not stopped at romantic attachments. At Zelesz in 1818, there had been Pepi Pöckelhofer, one of the Countess's housemaids, *very pretty, and often pays me a visit*, he had written to his friends, and he was acquainted with other women as accommodating as Pepi, as attractive, no doubt, but alas! less healthy. In 1823 he fell ill: the symptoms were unmistakably those of syphilis.

Perhaps, to drown his sorrow, he drank at this time more than was wise, but he does not deserve because of it to be called a drunkard – for how could any man addicted to drink have been able to achieve such a considerable output in so few years?

He worked with exemplary regularity every morning from six or seven o'clock to noon or one o'clock. As soon as he had finished a composition, he started at once on another. This disengagement from the completed work, the lack of enthusiasm for the object achieved, are characteristic of the creative mind, whose activity constantly renews itself, deriving fresh impetus from the successive creations to which it gives life, and from which it withdraws as soon as each is completed:

Stroll in town: lithograph by Moritz von Schwind. Schwind seated on the right, behind him Schubert next to Vogl; Schober behind them, raising his hat. →

Schubert, Lachner, Schwind and Vogl sing a serenade.

Lachner, Schubert and von Bauernfeld at Grinzing.

an apparent faithlessness betokening the artist's faith in himself. It was doubtless also from conscientiousness, the creator's integrity towards himself and his creation, that Schubert's manuscripts were models of care, craftsmanship and precision: they are nearly always dated.

Moritz von Schwind describes how Schubert spent his time. After a morning devoted to composition, 'it was his custom to go to the café and read the papers; he liked too, in the fine season, to wander about the countryside with a friend. He was a great lover of the theatre, as fond of opera as of comedy. Evening gatherings were at 'The Black Cat' or 'The Snail', or the favourite 'Crown of Hungary', all places where he found healthy relaxation. He drank readily, though none ever saw him drunk. He seemed to ponder over his drink with a faraway look, or he would exchange pleasantries, surrendering himself to the ease and good fellowship of the occasion.'

At these times he would drink beer, wine when he had the money, and liked not only the wines of the Viennese vineyards, but the Heurige sold locally at the houses hung with wreaths of fir, and Hungarian wines, Tokay and Szegzard, and the Styrian Schilcher. As the inn is the wanderer's hearth, so Schubert's friends were his

Lachner's farewell concert. Schubert applauding in the front row.

family; mellowed by the wine, he fancied himself happy – an illusion fostered by his youth, charm and gaiety, and those of his circle of friends as lively as himself.

Schubert was not over-particular as to his personal relationships – and the hazards and promiscuities of bohemian life are well known. But he had the secret of making and keeping true, devoted friends, the enthusiasts who formed his faithful circle and transformed his life.

They were Hüttenbrenner, Senn, Hartmann, Mayrhofer, Spaun, Vogl, Kupelwieser, Bauernfeld, Lachner, Schwind. As Walter Dahms has written: 'They were happy adolescents who, in this kindly imperial city, were out for as much pleasure as could be found. With an abundant zest for life, they rose above the pettinesses of existence. Whatever their diversity of mind, their chosen direction, they were united in the common bond of the promise and preparation of their lives' fulfilment, and in their love of the arts and sciences.' Numbered in their ranks were poets, painters, philosophers, but no composer: Schubert sufficed. 'Through him', wrote Spaun, 'we are all friends'.

Sketches by Moritz von Schwind,
made on the occasion of Lachner's Jubilee.
(He was Court conductor at Munich.)

Bohemian life is transitory; its devotees forsake it or die in it: none stays. There is no sight more pathetic than an old bohemian. Schubert's friends looked confidently to the future; and some of them achieved considerable success.

Their gatherings were not only at inns, but also at each other's houses, at the painter, Ludwig Mohn's, at Bruchmann's, most frequently at Schober's.

Jenger, Hüttenbrenner and Schubert. *(Pastel drawing by J. Teltscher, 1827.)*

Schubert's music was performed, the wives and sweethearts of the merry crew were invited, and all joined in dancing in the lighthearted revels that became known as the 'Schubertiads'.

There were also readings with discussions on literature and philosophy, and, though rarely, on politics. From Franz von Hartmann's journal we have a list of the works read and studied at Schober's during the winter of 1827–1828: Goethe's *Faust*, *Pandora*, and *The Green Snake*, the occult tale that they must have found a tough nut to crack; the second volume of Heine's *Impressions of Travel*, the principal dramas and novels of Kleist, Tieck's tales, the poems of Schlegel, Shakespeare, and the then-fashionable Ossian and Scott.

By this list, it is evident that Schubert was acquainted with

A 'Schubertiad' in progress at Atzenbrugg.

the much-discussed romantic works of his time, and that without being an 'intellectual', he kept well abreast of current literary output. In view of this, it is the more surprising that he should never have included in his musical settings the folk poems collected by Arnim and Brentano in *Des Knaben Wunderhorn*, which would seem so congenial to his thought.

The scene of a charade, 'The Fall'. Schubert at the piano. Schober as the Serpent twines himself round the Tree of Good and Evil (Kupelwieser); in front of them Adam (Jenger) presenting the apple to Eve. Spaun seated on the right.

Schubert's life at this time, distinguished by no eccentricity of habit or appearance, differed in no respect from that of a good many of his Viennese contemporaries of about the year 1825. Busy producing the foremost works of musical romanticism, he did not feel it incumbent upon him to impress people with behaviour that was anything but normal. With the true greatness that spurns the meretricious, faithful to the ideals of German

The Songs of Ossian, first edition.

romanticism which lay primarily in its supreme elevation of the emotions, the ideal expression of man's inner self, he abhorred ostentation and a reputation that was in any way spurious.

The French Romantics, especially the cranks of 1820 and the 'Young France' movement of 1830, captivated by Byron's excesses, tried to imitate him, believing in good faith that romanticism consists of actions and modes of behaviour. Dressing themselves up in Renaissance costume, growing their hair and beards long, drinking toasts to life from skulls and pursuing the outrageous with remarkable persistence, they lost sight, as they did so, of the romantic fundamental: its function from within, its power to affect and change both heart and outlook.

Thus, while they postured, Schubert composed in 1828 the work that might well be termed the charter of romantic music, his *Quintet in C major*, (*Op.* 163) for two violins, viola and two cellos.

Alfred de Musset, by Dévéria.

Franz Schubert.

(Drawing by Moritz von Schwind.)

Great Expectations

1797-1818

There are three books that have a bearing not only upon Schubert's life, but perhaps also, upon the life of each one of us: Dickens' *Great Expectations*, Goethe's *Wilhelm Meister*, and Balzac's *Les Illusions Perdues*.

Schubert's father leaves it on record: 'In the course of his fifth year I was preparing him for the elementary class, and in his sixth year I sent him to school, where he was regularly placed first. Since his earliest childhood he loved company, and was never gayer than when he could spend his leisure with merry companions.'

His father also taught him the violin, so that he soon gained a degree of proficiency in playing easy duos. His brother Ignaz, twelve years his senior, and already assistant master in his father's school, taught him the piano. Both soon recognised that theirs was no ordinary pupil. His father continues: 'I was amazed to find that after a few months he had no further need of my lessons, and could study on his own. In fact, he was soon so advanced that I had to recognise that he had far outstripped me and had achieved a mastery to which I should never attain.'

And so he was entrusted to the hands of a more expert teacher, Michael Holzer, choirmaster of the Lichtenthal church, who

Franz Schubert in the uniform of the Convict School.

instructed him in singing, the viola, organ and thorough-bass, and gave him his first harmony lessons. At the age of eleven he distinguished himself in singing soprano in the Lichtenthal church. The child took to transposing, elaborating, improvising on a given theme, and Holzer found himself already rewarded by his progress. 'He positively has music in his little finger' he remarked with enthusiasm, and determined to give him all the help in his power. Now and then Schubert deputised for his master at the organ, and did it so well that Holzer ceased to teach him only when he had imparted to him the whole store of his own wide learning, a debt Schubert acknowledged later in the dedication of one of his Masses.

In May 1808 two vacancies for boys occurred in the choir of the Imperial Chapel; and on 1 October Franz passed the entrance test in a grey cloth suit. His voice was flexible and well developed, and he was admitted as a small angelic chorister, being classed as one of the two best boy sopranos by Salieri, the Court Kapellmeister, Mozart's former rival. Salieri, in fact, was so impressed with the boy's musicianship that there was no difficulty about securing Franz's admission as a boarder to the 'Stadtkonvikt'.

The Imperial Convict, in effect a sort of Conservatorium, was a school attached to the University, where the ten little Court choristers received their education. In the heart of Vienna, on premises formerly the property of the Jesuits, closed in 1785 by the Emperor Joseph II, re-opened in 1802 by his successor the Emperor Franz II, under the direction of brothers of the Piarist Order, this was the college that was to be Schubert's prison from 1808 to 1813, from his twelfth to his seventeenth year. His prison, because the building was cold, damp and forbidding, and the discipline severe, and the child dreamed longingly of the happiness of home, the loving company of his brothers, the Lich-

Salieri.

The Stadtkonvikt (the Convict), Vienna.

tenthal gardens, and his good master Holzer. He became serious and reserved.

But the Convict was also his guiding star, for there he studied the secondary subjects that cultivated his innate feeling for poetry, opening to him the door to Goethe's works at an age when lighter reading would otherwise be more usual – and above all, because there he could practise, and deepen his musical understanding.

His professors complained at times of his lack of diligence in some subjects, but never, it is safe to assume, in music, for which his reports show an unusual talent and special distinction.

In addition to singing, the compulsory study of the angelic choirboys, musical training at the Convict included ensemble, chamber music and symphony. Franz's special joy was playing the violin in the orchestra. To this he added his discovery of the new joy of composing, and the personal joy of his friendship with Joseph von Spaun, who was nine years his senior, studying law preparatory to leaving the college, and the first of the friends who were to be Schubert's companions for the rest of his life.

In Spaun's memoirs we have this account of Franz's life at the Convict:

'The institution did not seem to suit him, for the little boy was always grave and uncommunicative. As he already played the violin pretty well, he played in the small orchestra which performed a symphony and an overture most evenings, often with a remarkable degree of success for such young players. As leader of the second violins, I was sitting, while little Schubert played standing behind me, overlooking the same copy. I soon noticed that this little musician was playing with far more assurance than myself. My interest aroused, I noticed how eagerly the child entered into the fine symphonies we were playing. One day, I found him alone in the music room, sitting at the piano, which, although his fingers were small, he already played extremely well. He was studying a sonata by Mozart, and told me that he liked it, but that he found Mozart difficult. As I asked him in a friendly way to play to me, he played a minuet of his own composition. He started shyly and blushing at first, but was cheered by my praise. He told me that he often secretly translated his thoughts into sound, but that his father must not know, as he was absolutely against his devoting himself to music.'

In 1811, as a young lawyer, Spaun revisited Vienna and eager to see his former classmates again, made a pilgrimage to his old haunts at the Convict.

'I found my young friend somewhat grown, and in good spirits', he reports. 'He had for some time been the leader of the orchestra, in whose ranks he was held in respect, and with whom he had some influence in programme matters. Schubert then told me that he had already composed a great many pieces: a sonata, a fantasy, a small opera, and that he was going to write a Mass. His chief difficulty was that as he had no manuscript music paper or money to buy any, he had first to trace lines upon ordinary paper, which also he did not always know how to get. So I gave him an ample supply of music paper, of which he used an amazing quantity. He wrote with remarkable speed, and spent his study hours, which he found all too short, in composing tirelessly.'

His earliest friendships date from the college; besides Spaun, among his classmates were Stadler, Holzapfel, Kenner, Bibl, and in all probability, Nestroy and the future Cardinal Rauscher. All of them made good in the world; Schubert himself was marked out for another destiny.

Joseph von Spaun, after Kupelwieser.

For the time-being, besides playing in the orchestra under the direction of Wenzel Ruciczka, he sometimes also took his place on the rostrum, and although he never became a good conductor, he acquired in this way a more thorough knowledge of symphonic music. Though Ruciczka included in his programmes works by composers who were his fellow Moravians, young Schubert turned instinctively to the great masters and the finest music: to Haydn, Mozart, Beethoven. He had also a taste for Méhul.

Schubert's earliest compositions date from 1810: the *Fantasy in G* for piano duet (erroneously called *Leichenphantasie* or *Corpse-Fantasia*) written between 8 April and 1 May 1810 at the age of thirteen; a *String Quartet in G* of which only two movements survive; a sketch of material for the second and third movements of the *Second Quartet in C major*, written in September 1812; an *Overture* with trumpets and cymbals; and his first experiment in a song-form he was to make famous in the *lied*, *Hagar's Lament*, the setting of a poem by Schücking, dated 30 March 1811. At about this time, the *Ballades* of Zumsteeg made a great impression on Schubert, and according to Spaun, his intention was to set *Hagar's Lament*, which Zumsteeg had published in 1797, in its contemporary style – an essay in imitation of the kind valuable to composition students in the foundation of technique.

This song was followed by *The Maiden's Lament*, on a poem by Schiller, and *The Parricide* by Pfeffel, 26 December 1811. From 1812 onwards he produced an ever-increasing number of works, among them a sketch for an Operetta in 3 acts on a text by Kotzebue, *Der Spiegelritter*, (*The Looking-glass Knight*); overtures for orchestra and for piano; minuets; a *Salve Regina in A*; a *Kyrie*; the first two string quartets, (known as of Series V); and a *Trio in B flat* for violin, cello and piano, which was not published until 1923.

Schubert's father was alarmed at such fertility on the part of his son, who, in order to give rein to his inspiration, was neglecting other tasks so as not to spare a moment from music. At this point the first disputes arose between Schubert and his father, for whom music was no more than a relaxation, at most a holiday diversion. For Franz, it was his life, and life itself. The schoolmaster expected his son to become a respectable official like his brothers and himself, and to practise music as a leisure accomplishment. But Franz felt himself an artist elect, and had no intention of being relegated to the cautious ranks of amateurs who were 'weekend musicians'. He had faith in his powers, drawing from them courage, pride and conviction.

As he composed more and more, his college reports became worse. To his father, the reason was evident. There followed renewed outbursts, fresh bans upon composing, indeed, according to Schubert's autobiographical account, *My Dream*, of 3 July 1822, it seems that he was turned out of his father's house. If this is the correct interpretation of Schubert's account (one that we owe to Aloïs Fellner, cited in the monograph by Walter Dahms), Franz must have felt it keenly. There were no more happy Sundays or happy family reunions when he basked in the warmth of home and played chamber music with his father and brothers, the quartets in which Ferdinand, three years older then he, played first violin, Ignaz, second violin, Franz himself the viola, and their father the cello. When his father made a mistake, as he often did, Franz would pretend not to notice, then, at a fresh error, he would remark respectfully: 'My Herr Father, there must be something wrong there.' From the gloomy duress of the college the boy looked back upon these happy times, re-living their joys with a heavy heart.

Before long he had cause for greater grief. On 28 May 1812 his mother died of typhoid. Sorrow softened Herr Schubert, and father and son were reconciled by the bier of the mother whose good, devoted life had been lived in quietness and self-effacement.

Thenceforth Schubert was allowed to continue his studies in composition, and his father placed him with Salieri, who until 1817, taught him counterpoint and vocal technique. Salieri would have liked him to admire the eighteenth century Italian composers, and was vexed at his pupil's preference for Haydn, Mozart and above all, Beethoven, whom Salieri himself regarded as a dangerous crank. At the same time, he recognised Schubert's talent and encouraged him, and Schubert was fortunate in having the college orchestra as well as his family quartet with which to try out his early works as he wrote them, so that he could assess effects, correct, improve and experiment.

Meanwhile, he left college in 1813, at the end of the school year. His father wished him to continue his studies, and he was allowed to stay on at the Convict on condition that he made progress in mathematics. But Schubert, weary of any control other than the self-imposed discipline of his own talent, would never recognise any rule except that of obedience to the laws of his own being; and the man traditionally depicted as so modest, shy and simple, proved himself capable of struggling in his childhood against his father's authority, in his adolescence against worldly distractions, and in his early maturity against the powerful temptations of doubt and despair. For all his retiring mien, there was in him something indomitable, drawn from the innermost resources of his being, that compelled him to escape from constraint, whether of family, college or society. Schubert had staked all upon unworldly values, the intoxication of art; nothing else mattered to him, be it wealth, honours, vanities, pleasures. To him, his art was an act of faith to which all else was sacrificed. From it sprang his free bohemian ways, his incessant wanderlust, his unconcern about money, security and background: his real life was elsewhere. He lived among his friends, first with one, then with another, sharing a room with Mayrhofer, Schober or Spaun; content with a hired piano, the Fröhlich family library, the art treasures of the Austrian churches and monasteries round about. His real possessions were the forest streams, the moonlight nights in the woods, whose enchantment he sings so exquisitely in *Nachtgesang im Walde*, (*Forest Nocturne*), *Op. 139b.* 1827, for male voice chorus and four horns. All that is uplifting and inspired in the poetic concept of nature and in the spontaneous outpouring of romantic beauty, he made especially his own; therein lies his particular claim to immortality.

In the meantime, after his indifferent college record of 1813, he did not complete his studies there, and rather than submit to a fourteen years' term of military service, he agreed to take a teacher's training course at the Normal School of St. Anna, where at least he would be able to go on composing.

He did not leave the college empty handed. In addition to his output of the years 1810, 1811 and 1812, he produced between April and July 1813 trios, canons, settings of poems by Schiller, a *Wind Octet* which survives only in its Minuet and Finale, a *Drinking Song* for bass solo, male voice chorus and piano, the *Fourth, Fifth and Sixth String Quartets*, and a *Cantata* for his father's name-day, for two tenors, bass, and guitar accompaniment, written in September 1813, and performed 4 October of that year in his father's house at the Sign of 'The Black Horse', on the patronal feast of St. Francis. As his voice was breaking, he played the guitar, while his brothers sang. He had lost his angelic boyish soprano, and had to content himself for the rest of

(C. D. Friedrich, 1812.)

The Normal School of St. Anna.

his days with 'a weak tenor', though he knew how to make capable use of it in the vocal quartets that were such a popular feature of Viennese life at the time.

The school of St. Anna, for the training of teachers, had been founded in the reign of the Empress Maria-Theresa by Joseph Mesmer, brother of the more famous Mesmer, Franz Anton, the magnetist. The course lasted about six months. Schubert followed it between the end of October 1813 till 19 August 1814, a period that was not musically wasted, as he completed on 28 October 1813 his *Symphony No. 1 in D major*, which he dedicated to Dr. Lang, Director of the Convict, and wrote also a collection of Minuets and Allemandes for orchestra, and thirty Minuets for piano. His early *String Quartet No. 10 in E flat major*, (*Op. 125, No. 1*) belongs also to this period.

In 1814 followed *String Quartet No. 7 in D major*, settings of poems by the lugubrious Matthisson, and his *Mass in F major*, at which he was working from 17 May to 22 June, and which was first heard on 16 October in the Lichtenthal church when his dear Theresa sang the soprano part. Since he had entered the Normal School he had also sketched out a 3-act opera on a text by Kotzebue, *Des Teufels Lustschloss* (*The Devil's Pleasure Palace*), which he revised, although ineffectually, on Salieri's advice.

By the autumn of 1814 he had his secondary Teacher's Diploma, a matter of satisfaction to his father, a number of immature works, as full of youthful ardour as his first symphony, and the experience of his first love.

It was undoubtedly only for the lack of an opening elsewhere that he joined his father's school in the Säulengasse, in the autumn of 1814, as his assistant, a post in which he still felt the pressure of his father's authority. It may have been that by showing himself willing to submit thus far, he hoped he might more easily gain Theresa's hand: at any rate, the poor young lover had no other opportunities, and found himself teaching youngsters of five and six years old, unruly, disobedient little fiends whom he did not hesitate to correct. 'It is true', he remarks to Lachner, 'every time I tried to compose, the little blackguards irritated me so much that I lost my train of thought, so naturally I gave them a good hiding.'

The young master could not have had the patience for the job, conscious, as he was, that he had better things to do than to teach the alphabet to young animals inclined only for noise, freedom and the open air. It was too much to expect respect for creative work on the part of children, themselves as insistent on their way as the artist must be on his. Schubert's first need was for the silence necessary for the inner music that sang within him.

Nonetheless, his work was carried on in spite of them. On 5 September 1814, carried away by his sense of his own powers, he wrote at the end of the first movement of his *Quartet in B flat major* (*Op. 160*), the words 'Written in a few hours'; and by 19 October, the astonishing achievement of his setting of Goethe's poem *Gretchen am Spinnrade* shows the immediate perfection of his mastery as a song-writer. In this song are the same characteristics that we admire in the later *Schöne Müllerin*

Schubert at seventeen.
(Drawing by Schober)

and *Winterreise:* the same perfect merging of words and music, the contrast between the simplicity of the melody and the complexity of the accompaniment and its daring modulations. Here we see a composer of seventeen giving full play to his melodic inspiration with complete assurance: his establishment as a mature artist, his inception of the German Lied, which he was later to bring to fruition.

One wonders if he was conscious of this creation? At all events, the ensuing year to the end of 1815 was the most prolific of his life, one that justified all his 'Great Expectations', and that contained four operas, his first and second symphonies, his second and third Masses, the *String Quartet No. 9 in G minor*, two piano sonatas, sacred and secular choral works, many miscellaneous piano pieces, and one hundred and forty Lieder, including the great *Erlkönig*. Spaun describes in his memoirs Schubert's trance-like condition when this wonderful song seemed to be dictated to him by his creative spirit, as if by a psychic phenomenon: 'One afternoon I went with Mayrhofer to see Schubert, who was then living at his father's house in the Himmelpfortgrund. We found him glowing, impassioned, in the middle of reading aloud from a book called *The Erl King*. After striding up and down, book in hand, he sat down all of a sudden, and in no time the great song was on paper. As Schubert had no piano, we rushed to the Convict, and there, the very same evening, *The Erl King* was first sung and acclaimed. Then Ruciczka, the aged Court Organist, played it over again to himself, without the voice, examining it closely and lovingly in every detail, profoundly moved by what he found there. As some of those

Manuscript of 'Gretchen am Spinnrade'.

present were disposed to be critical of a certain recurring dissonance, Ruciczka, illustrating at the piano as he went, explained how inevitably it matched a passage in the poem, and with what beauty it was brought to a satisfying resolution.'

In 1816, Schubert was still contemplating marriage, though the thought of it for him, as a free man, was a formidable one, and he had only an annual salary of 40 fl. with which to set up house. It was necessary for him to be ambitious for Theresa if not for himself, and as towards the end of 1815, the post had fallen vacant of Professor at the Government School of Music at Laibach, (now Ljubljana in Yugoslavia), Schubert applied for it, hoping for the recommendation of Salieri. But Salieri, although he gave Schubert a testimonial, backed another candidate.

It seemed foreordained that Schubert was not to go to Laibach, and that he was not to marry Theresa. Moreover, he was unfitted for marriage, and he knew it. He was reluctant to tie himself for always: his natural affections did not usurp for long the place of music. From this time, he had made his choice. Perhaps Theresa herself may have realised the dangers and limitations of the young composer's love; it would account for her engagement in 1819, when her father was no longer living and she was not subject to anyone's control, to an obscure man with whom she hoped to find happiness.

Throughout 1816, Schubert worked without respite, and produced many songs, the *Fourth Symphony*, that he called 'The Tragic', a String Trio in one movement, the *String Quartet No. 11 in E major* (*Op. 125, No. 2*), an attractive *Rondo in*

Manuscript of '*Erlkönig*'.

A major for solo violin and string quartet, and the three *Sonatinas for Violin and Piano* (*Op. 137*, *Nos. 1*, *2 and 3*).

In the diary that he kept – unfortunately for us – only irregularly, there is the following entry for 17 June 1816: *Today for the first time, I composed for money. A cantata ... The fee is 100 fl.* – a sum more than twice his annual salary.

Meanwhile, a meeting was effected between the distinguished singer Vogl, then at the height of his fame, and Schubert, who were invited by Schober to meet at his house. At first Vogl showed little enthusiasm, but when he had sung *Schäfers Klagelied* and *Ganymed*, his mood changed. On leaving, he tapped Schubert on the shoulder, remarking: 'There is something in you; but you are too little of an actor, too little of a charlatan. You squander your fine ideas instead of making the most of them.'

So imbued was he with Schubert's genius that instead of retiring as he had planned, he took up his career afresh, and made it his special mission to spread his new friend's renown throughout Vienna.

It was thus that Vogl became the greatest interpreter of Schubert's songs, and, in company with Spaun, Schober and Mayrhofer, one of his staunchest, keenest and most helpful friends.

In Vogl's journal there is a reference to what he describes felicitously as Schubert's musical clairvoyance: 'The lack of a good school of singing has never been more plainly shown than by Schubert's songs. Otherwise, what an amazing and far-reaching impact would be made wherever the German tongue is known, by these truly divine compositions, these utterances of musical second sight! How many would understand, perhaps for the first time, the full import of text, poetry in music, words in harmonic setting, thoughts revealed afresh in music?'

It would be hard to find a better definition of the lied.

In the course of 1816 Schubert made considerable strides in the development of his pianistic style, and produced at this period the six *Piano Sonatas* full of beauty and poise: *No. 4 in A minor*, *No. 6 in D flat major*, *No. 7 in F sharp minor*, *No. 8 in E major*, *No. 9 in A flat major*. He composed also some sixty songs, among them, *Lob der Thränen* (*The Praise of Tears*), *Der Tod und das Mädchen* (*Death and the Maiden*), *An die Musik*, *Die Forelle* (*The Trout*), and the first version of his setting of

Theresa Grob

Goethe's *Gesang der Geister über den Wassern* (*Song of the Spirits across the Waters*).

His father obtained for him a year's leave, and he found himself free of the school he hated, free of his family home, now congested since his father's second marriage to a step-mother who was bearing child after child, and free from a love that had begun to weigh heavily upon him. In January 1817 he reached the age of twenty, having served his apprenticeship, eager to try his strength in a wider field. Spaun and Schober begged him to allow them to undertake the management of his career. Up to now, everything had conspired to further the development of his gifts.

Victor Hugo, when he was twelve years old, wrote in one of his notebooks: 'Be Chateaubriand or nothing' – and Schubert cherished dreams as ambitious, though he expressed them less forcefully. He remarked to Spaun, who predicted a fine future for him: *In my heart I hope very much to make something of myself, but who can ever do anything after Beethoven?*

It was with the high hope of following Beethoven that he left his father's house at the end of 1817. All was still possible, the best of life was still to come.

Vogl and Schubert (Caricature by Schober.)

Vogel und Franz Schubert ziehen aus zu Kampf

Title page: Variations for Pianoforte Duet, Op. 10, dedicated to Beethoven.

Franz von Schober in 1821, by Kupelwieser.

(Moritz von Schwind)

Wilhelm Meister's Apprenticeship

1818–1824

First of all it was necessary that Schubert should know the world. A chance came through the good offices of his friend Johann Unger, who introduced him to Count Esterhazy – not the Count Nicolas who had been Haydn's famous patron, nor his son, Paul-Antonius, but Count Johann, of another branch of the family.

This nobleman had two daughters, of whom Marie, the elder, then aged thirteen, had a 'very lovely soprano voice'. Schubert gave her music lessons. Caroline, the younger, was only eleven. All the family sang and played, parents as well as children, and Schubert accepted joyfully the invitation to spend the summer of 1818 with them at the castle of Zelesz in Hungary. It was the first time he had been out of Austria.

For the first weeks of this Hungarian summer he was deliriously happy. He was in the country again, among fields and woods; he lived well with the servants, at whose table he ate, and made a good impression on his employers, particularly on the young Countesses. It was not until his second visit there six years later that he fell in love with Caroline, – indeed, in 1818 he may perhaps have been more attracted by their mother, who was young and extremely personable, though

Franz Schubert.
(Miniature by Robert Theer, 1829.)

Caroline, Albert and Marie Esterhazy.

this did not prevent his taking notice of Pepi, her pretty chambermaid. He had obviously plenty to do, and wrote only a few songs, among them, *Einsamkeit* (*Solitude*), a setting of a poem by Mayrhofer, *Das Marienbild* (*Portrait of Marie*), *Der Blumenbrief* (*The Flowers' Message*), and the delightful *Litaney auf das Fest aller Seelen* (*Litany of All Souls Day*), together with some piano pieces for two and four hands. According to Spaun, the *Variations on a French Song, Reposez-vous, bon Chevalier* (*Op. 10*), which he subsequently dedicated to Beethoven, also date from his first visit to Zelesz. Of remarkable originality, they are known to have pleased Beethoven, who played them with his nephew Carl.

But the Esterhazys prolonged their holidays, and Schubert began to pine. He longed for Vienna and its life, his friends,

The Castle of Zelesz.

Excursion of the 'Schubertianer' in 1829, by Kupelwieser. Schubert standing upright on the carriage step.

the theatres and cafés, and it was not until the end of November that he returned to his beloved city.

He had earned some money, and as the school term had long since begun, he assumed himself dismissed, and was glad. But his father thought otherwise, wondering what his son would live on, and Franz sent in a request for re-admission to the Rossau school staff, as 'sixth assistant'. The plan came to nothing: Schubert never resumed the school yoke, and one can only imagine his father's chagrin. But Schubert was nearly twenty-two, and he was adamant. He was a free man, an artist elect, and a born musician. He was undaunted by poverty; freedom and leisure meant more than money to him – and for the second time, his father turned him out of the house.

Schober took him in, and from thenceforth the homeless Schubert went from one to another, from Schober to Mayrhofer, from Mayrhofer to Spaun and back to Schober again, finally, to his brother Ferdinand to die. He lived with his friends in furnished rooms, as indifferent to his personal comforts as he was determined on the dedication of his life to music.

The years that followed held nothing of note. He followed his routine of mornings devoted to work, afternoons and evenings of friendship, outings and strolls. He went into society when he thought it would be helpful to his career, but never felt himself at ease there, preferring the frank, friendly circles of the poets, musicians and artists who are the happiest of all companions, and were his spiritual family. It was thus that from 1819 he took to visiting the home of the Fröhlich sisters. There were four of them: Barbara drew, Josephine sang, Anna and Catherine played the piano. Catherine was known also for her attachment to the poet and dramatist Grillparzer, with whom she allied herself in perpetual betrothal. All four were lively, charming and attractive, and Schubert became their friend and confidant.

The new friend who took him to their house, and who was almost as decisive an influence in his life as the singer Vogl, was Ignaz von Sonnleithner, a keen music-lover who knew all the musicians and was their protector and friend, and to whom Beethoven bequeathed his papers. At one of the fortnightly concerts he had founded, he arranged in January 1819 a performance of *Prometheus*, a commissioned cantata of Schubert's, since lost. On 1 December of that year, August von Gymnich, a young singer no less enthusiastic than Sonnleithner, carried away his fashionable audience with *Erlkönig*, and Schubert's

Grillparzer.

Catherine Fröhlich.

Josephine Fröhlich.

Sonnleithner.

name became known in the upper circles of Viennese society.

Early in 1821, Gymnich gave the first performance of *The Wanderer*, setting of a poem by August Wilhelm von Schlegel, 1819, and at a select gathering at Gundelhof, Sonnleithner's beautiful home in the Bauermarkt, where he kept open house to all people of culture, *Gretchen am Spinnrade*, *Der Jüngling auf dem Hügel* (*The Young Man on the Mountain*) and other lieder were performed. He arranged for the performances of yet others at a concert of a Welfare Society run by ladies of the aristocracy, and at concerts of the Society of the Friends of Music, evening parties given by artists, and charity performances at the Kärntnerthor theatre; and it was thus that *An die Nachtigall* (*To the Nightingale*), a setting of words by Johann Unger for vocal quartet, piano and guitar made a conspicuously successful début on 22 April 1821. Finally, thanks to Spaun, Schubert's music began to receive performances further afield, at Linz and Graz.

Luck was with him, his name and reputation prospered, his friends effectually helped his cause. But in spite of it he felt disheartened, because his music had not succeeded with the world at large or the influential circles of upper class Vienna, each of them inimical to his efforts. Schubert's music was in advance of its time: it was unorthodox, disconcerting, and the public prefers what it knows.

By 1820 he had a following of only a limited progressive circle of admirers, who were inadequate when it came to securing official backing or influence with publishers – whose first consideration, in any case, is a commercial one. Schubert's qualified success must have wounded him: he was not the man to sit down under it.

He needed to find a publisher: it was his only hope of extending his audience and assuring his future.

The piano has been called the supreme romantic instrument; it certainly surpasses the harp and guitar, both of them equally popular at the beginning of the nineteenth century. The favourite répertoire of the young ladies of 1820 was caprices, rondos and variations, 'fantaisies brillantes', tarantellas and minuets, and fashionable operatic selections. Schubert offered them long, serious sonatas, andantes, allegros, marches, and a year or two later, impromptus and moments musicaux. They did not conform to popular taste, and although they were later to form it, editorial refusal is understandable. Young persons of 1820 preferred

Gundelhof, the Sonnleithners' house in the Bauermarkt.

A Schubert soirée at Joseph von Spaun's.

Schubert at the piano accompanying Vogl. Mayrhofer standing extreme right. Above the piano, a portrait of Caroline Esterhazy.

(Sepia by Moritz von Schwind.)

Steibelt, Hummel, Cramer and the Italians, Mozart sometimes, Bach never. But although Schubert composed also dozens of lighter pieces of a more popular type – numerous Ecossaises, Ländler, gallops and other dances, as well as quantities of works for piano duet such as overtures, polonaises, fantaisies, variations and divertissements, none of them was printed until after his death.

After a delay of three months, a letter dated 12 November 1822 from the great publisher Peters of Leipzig to Hüttenbrenner, who had written to put forward Schubert as a second Beethoven, brought the reply – which is as pertinent for young composers of today as it was then – that Peters had heard favourably of Schubert's songs, but that an editor must 'consider popular taste rather than that of a minority', and that 'although he was committed to publish the works of Spohr, Romberg, Hummel etc., he was nevertheless interested in the discovery of unknown composers.' But he still did not accept Schubert, giving as his reason 'I must honour my obligations to already known composers, and if I find them sufficiently lucrative, I must perforce leave to others the task of bringing forward the unknown.' He assures his correspondent that 'directly a composer has made his name and his works are recognised, I am his man, as in that case his works become eligible for publication under my scheme, in which honour is above profit...'

Comment is superfluous on this testimony of bad faith and exploitation, and Cappi and Diabelli, Sauer and Leidesdorf were no more honest, though they did publish Schubert. Cappi and Diabelli accepted in 1821 Sonnleithner's proposal that the songs should be published by subscription under separate titles, a series which opened with *Der Erlkönig* as *Op. 1*, and was immediately subscribed. *Op. 2*, *Gretchen am Spinnrade* and *Op. 3*, *Des Schäfers Klaglied*, *Meeresstille* (*Becalmed*), *Heidenröslein* and *Jägers Abendlied* (*Hunter's Night Song*) followed, and others that continued the series as far as the ninth volume which contained – appropriately at this period of the popularity of carnival – the collected waltzes. The publishers took half the rights, assigning the other half to Schubert, a fairly substantial sum in which can be seen the reason for Peters' reference to his 'favourable' knowledge of him as a song-writer.

Meanwhile, Schubert had to bear the brunt of Diabelli's hard bargaining. Poor and unbusinesslike, he allowed him to have *The Wanderer Fantasy* for 50 fl., and for a paltry sum, the exclusive rights of eighteen other works already published.

Shocked and angry, Schubert approached Sauer and Leidesdorf, who published in 1823 his Lieder Op. 21, 22 and 23. But his finances were in no better shape, ravaged as they were by the extravagances of his bohemianism, in which he was the prey of cafés and restaurants. Between 1818 and 1828 he earned enough to keep himself from want, and did not suffer the hunger and need that legend has ascribed to him. His impecuniousness was largely because when he was in funds he spent them as lavishly on his friends as on himself, and although himself helped financially by Spaun, Schober and Vogl, he gave help in his turn to the painter Moritz von Schwind who joined his intimate circle in 1821, and the writer Eduard von Bauernfeld, both of them artists who were poorer than he. Only a hundred or so of his works, out of more than a thousand, were published in his lifetime, and of these the majority were songs. It was only at the end of the nineteenth century that the world received the revelation of his larger works.

Thus, his *Symphony No. 8 in B minor*, the famous *Unfinished*, whose manuscript is dated 30 October 1822, had to wait until 1865 for its performance. What irony! that this most loved and famous of Schubert's orchestral works, the most often recorded – a number running into several hundred discs – should have survived by a miracle.

So also, the *Mass in A flat*, his Missa Solemnis, one of all Schubert's works that is most deeply revealing of his spirit, and on which he was working between September 1819 and September 1822, was not published until 1875.

Succeeding generations have reserved a special affection for a third work he wrote at this time, *The Trout Quintet*, which he had at least the satisfaction of hearing.

Moritz von Schwind. Self portrait.

The circumstances that led him to write this simple, beautiful music, so full of youth and tenderness, are well known – a story as attractive as the work, and so, worth telling again.

In the summer of 1819 he went with Vogl on a tour of Styria in Upper Austria, and by 13 July was staying at Steyr with a typically keen Austrian music lover who was also an industrialist, Herr Joseph von Koller. *I am well,* writes Schubert to his brother Ferdinand. *In the house where I am staying there are eight young ladies, nearly all of them pretty. As you can imagine, there is plenty to do.* And forgetting, for the time-being, to gaze at the mountains and the green waters of the Steyr, he wrote for Josephine von Koller, *who is uncommonly pretty, plays the piano capitally and sings my songs,* the finest of his youthful piano sonatas, *Op. posth. 120 in A major,* whose very brevity contributes to its poetical charm and pianistic refinement, with an Andante comparable with Schubert's most moving song writing, and a folk song-like finale that is a characteristically happy blend of humour and simplicity, tenderness and fun. This work is in no way suggestive of the weighty sonatas of 1828, yet it foreshadows Schubert's second period, standing at a cross-roads in his career in its crystallisation of his style thus far, and in its anticipation of the future integration of style in the *Fifth Symphony in B flat* of 1816.

Herr von Koller was not the only musical enthusiast in Steyr. An amateur cellist, Silvester Paumgartner, who had a passion for chamber music and loved Schubert's song *The Trout,* asked him to write something, and so he wrote the *Quintet in A major* for the somewhat unusual combination of violin, viola, cello, double bass and piano, with a fourth movement composed of variations on the song, and containing a suitably important cello part.

The mood of the Andante recalls us to more serious thoughts – could it be the plaint of a forlorn lover, the reverie of one who is already aware that the joys of this world are not for him? Was it, as has been suggested, that he was thinking of Theresa, who had lately announced her betrothal?

The quintet, the true holiday music of happy amateurs, makes no pretensions beyond the expression of contentment and delight. Schubert is not preoccupied here with problems of form and balance, or with subtlety of style. It is natural music, that in its directness and easy grace breathes the joy of youth and creativity, making no other demands of us, bearing us along with it as the trout is borne by the swirling waters of the Steyr. We feel that nothing is imperilled yet, nothing lost. Schubert still cherished splendid dreams. The *Trout Quintet* recalls the impetuous vehemence of the early symphonies, the trustfulness of the *Salve Regina* of 1815; but it is no more than a recollection – already, in the second movement, a rift is perceptible. Schubert was sick at heart.

The Stage

Those who find themselves puzzled at Schubert's waste of time in troubling to compose so many operas, although he had no gift for lyric drama, are apt to discount the theatre's power of bestowing wealth and fame. It is not by chamber works and symphonies that a composer can hope to become famous: if he is realistic, he cannot but court the limelight – a fact particularly pertinent in the frivolous, victorious Vienna of the 1820's, where all that belonged to pleasure was rapturously received.

The drama, according to Mme. de Staël, the most social and mundane of the arts, offered a momentous choice. Schubert craved success, and who if not the world could bring it? The ambition was not unworthy of him. It was natural that a young artist, conscious of the ferment of his talent, should have aspired to oust the reigning clique at the opera, the Austrian composers who aped the Italians, and the Italians themselves. As Mozart had succeeded, why should not he?

The analogy with Wilhelm Meister is the more apposite as the first part of *Wilhelm Meister's Apprenticeship* was entitled *The Dramatic Mission of Wilhelm Meister.* It was among sophisticated people and actors that young Meister learned to develop his powers and find his own level among his fellow men. This world, this society that was to Werther the denial of self, the antithesis of emotion and desire, was to Meister the potential fulfilment of self, the source of culture, the aspiration toward a greater apprehension of the world and human intercourse. For such a purpose, Goethe could not have chosen a better vehicle than the stage. For Meister it was comedy, for Schubert it was opera; but circumstances do not change: the theatre is the medium in which mind,

The Leopoldstadt Theatre.

poetry and art are merged into a form of communal entertainment, the means of contact between the ideal, abstract sphere of the suffering artist, and the society in which he must take his place. It is a middle world, more real than reality, yet one in which actions take place as in actual life; in it we observe a convention that perpetuates and exaggerates all degrees of realism, the meeting point of humanity, art and adventure, the melting-pot wherein matter is rarefied into spirit.

It was difficult to see how Schubert could conquer Vienna except by the theatre. His more worldly friends encouraged him, with Spaun and Schober to help him make his way, Sonnleithner and Vogl to enlist all their connections. Thus spurred onward, supported by his friends, Schubert opened his campaign, and for several years from 1819, pursued it ardently. But the advantages that that good-natured, enterprising if rather

unstable young man Wilhelm Meister, derived from his experiences of the theatre, were scarcely to be reckoned as assets in Schubert's case, for beneath his diffident exterior, he had an already mature and discerning mind which, lacking in flexibility and insufficiently volatile, tended to turn inwards and retire into itself, so that while he strove to steel himself against the stage's more insidious lure, he was also repudiating those aspects of it that might have proved more helpful to him.

Meanwhile, he did not fail in patience and perseverance, as may be seen by the list of his dramatic works prepared by Otto Deutsch:

Des Teufels Lustschloss (*The Devil's Pleasure Palace*), opera in 3 acts. Kotzebue (1814).

Der Vierjährige Posten (*The Four Years' Sentry*), operetta in 1 act. Körner (1815).

Giboni in 'The Vestal Virgin' by Spontini.

Fernando, operetta in 1 act. Albert Stadler (1815).

Claudine von Villa Bella, (fragment), operetta in 3 acts. Goethe (1815).

Die Beiden Freunde von Salamanka (*The Two Friends from Salamanca*), operetta in 2 acts. Mayrhofer (1815).

Die Bürgschaft (*The Pledge*), (fragment), opera in 3 acts, 1816.

Adrast, miscellaneous numbers for an opera by Mayrhofer (1819?).

Die Zwillingsbrüder (*The Twin Brothers*), farce in 1 act. G. E. von Hofmann (1819).

Die Zauberharfe (*The Magic Harp*), overture and incidental music for a melodrama by G. E. von Hofmann (1820).

Two additional arias for *La Clochette Enchantée*, Hérold (1821).

Alfonso and Estrella, opera in 3 acts, von Schober (1822).
Der Häusliche Krieg (*The Domestic Campaign*), opera in 1 act, Castelli (1823).
Fierrabras, heroic-romantic opera in 3 acts, Joseph Kupelwieser (1823).
Rosamunde von Cypern (*Rosamunde of Cyprus*), incidental music for a drama by Helmine von Chézy (1823).

In addition he made sketches for *Der Spiegelritter* (*The Looking Glass Knight*), and *Die Minnesinger* on texts by Kotzebue, and in 1827, *Der Graf von Gleichen* (*The Count of Gleichen*), on a text by Bauernfeld.

He got his hand in with a fairy fantasy that earned Salieri's praise: *Des Teufels Lustschloss*, of which only the first act survives. The second was used to light the fire. We need not regret it.

In 1815 he produced no fewer than four dramatic works, two of them in 3 acts, and sketched three operettas, eight numbers for *Der Vierjährige Posten*, seven for *Fernando*, and seven for the first act of *Claudine*, of which the remaining acts were also used for fire-lighting. The Viennese were wildly enthusiastic about operetta, which appealed to their fondness for melodrama and airs in the Italian style, and Schubert, seeking to gratify their taste, made repeated attempts in this manner, which suited him even less than grand opera.

Spaun tells us that he was an inveterate play-goer: he loved it all, opera, straight drama or comedy. Since his college years he had heard *Iphigénia in Tauride* by Gluck, *Medea* by Cherubini, Mozart's *The Magic Flute*, *Jean de Paris* by Boieldieu, *The Swiss Family* by Weigl, as well as works by Paër, Mayr, Spontini, Méhul, Salieri, Rossini. The Convict had not wholly imprisoned him; as a child he had been stimulated by these pieces, and from an early age had conceived the desire to write for the theatre himself.

Up to 1819 it is difficult to distinguish Schubert's operettas from those of Paër, Mayr and even Salieri. They were honest, conservative compositions, without any particularly romantic characteristics, with dashing overtures in which lively play is made with woodwind and brass, pleasing airs and sprightly choruses. There was nothing new about them: it was only with the *Rosamunde* music that there appears Schubert the song-writer and composer of the piano pieces.

Despite the inadequacy of his libretti, Schubert's ambition was realized in 1820, when two of his dramatic works were mounted

– a remarkable achievement for a young, unknown composer. His friends had been tireless, particularly Vogl; and in view of the obstacles to be surmounted in order to get an opera accepted even by a known and honoured composer, these results were astonishing. The impossible became possible, Schubert's name was on all lips, he was entering into his heritage.

In 1820 his state of excitement, his daydreams, are imaginable. Never since autumn 1814 and the performance of his first Mass had he experienced such a thrill. It was not a question of love any more, but of the wooing of fame. As a young composer of 23, he was at last about to prove his destiny and show that fate had favoured him.

He knew it, and thought it a matter of course. For our own part, we commend the zeal of his friends, the extent of their contacts and their inexhaustible activity.

But disaster was to follow. Hüttenbrenner tells us that the première of *The Twin Brothers* at the old Kärntnerthor Theatre on 14 June 1820 had such a lukewarm reception that Schubert declined to take a bow in acknowledgement of the half-hearted applause, and the piece was taken off after six performances.

A home was found for the fantasies of *The Magic Harp* – a dangerous enough title after Mozart – at the An der Wien Theatre, where Hofmann, the librettist, was secretary. Schubert was sure of a performance, but it was his only assurance; he never saw the promised 500 gulden, his name did not appear on the posters, and this rather un-magic harp proved another fiasco, surviving for only eight performances. But Schubert had at least made contact with the directors of the theatre, and hoped to renew it, and after further efforts, he received in 1821 from Dietrichstein, the Director of the Imperial Opera, and Mosel the assistant director, a request for two additional numbers, a tenor aria and a comic duet for *La Clochette Enchantée* by Hérold. But this was the end of the matter. The authorities did not ask for more, Schubert's name was again omitted from the posters, and although his two numbers were the only ones applauded, the audience believed them to be by Hérold.

Undaunted, still imbued with faith and pertinacity, Schubert set to work on a libretto by his friend Schober, with whom he was lodging as the time. In the autumn, Schubert accompanied him to St.-Pölten, where the two worked together so congenially that Schober scarcely completed an act before Schubert set it to music, and the thirty-four numbers of *Alfonso and Estrella*

Anonymous portrait (Aldo Ciccolini Coll.)

begun 20 Sept. 1821, were completed the following February. But their zeal proved in vain, and the opera met with rejection in Vienna as well as in Dresden, where Weber had promised his support, though Schober did not drop the idea and followed up years later when he was travelling with Liszt, and persuaded him to stage the opera, which in the end received its first performance in an abridged version in Weimar 24 June 1854, under Liszt's own direction.

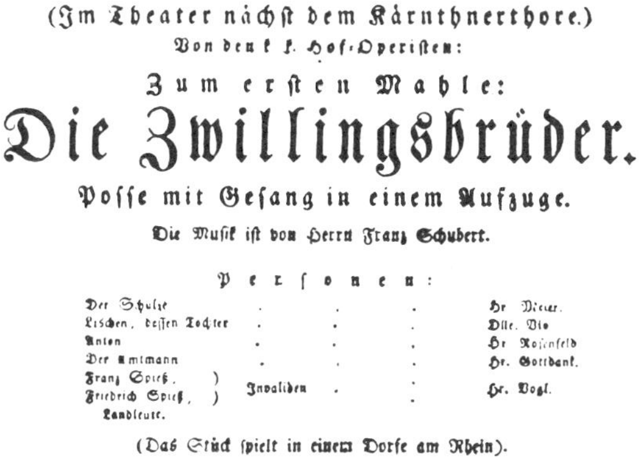

(Im Theater nächst dem Kärnthnerthore.)

Von den k. k. Hof-Operisten:

Zum ersten Mahle:

Die Zwillingsbrüder.

Posse mit Gesang in einem Aufzuge.

Die Musik ist von Herrn Franz Schubert.

Personen:

Der Schulze	. . .	Hr. Meier.
Lischen, dessen Tochter	. . .	Dlle. Vio
Anton	. . .	Hr. Rosenfeld
Der Amtmann	. . .	Hr. Gottdank.
Franz Spieß,) Friedrich Spieß,)	Invaliden . .	Hr. Vogl.
Landleute.		

(Das Stück spielt in einem Dorfe am Rhein).

Poster for 'The Twin Brothers'.

The development of Schubert's dramatic style is discernible in *Alfonso and Estrella*, as it is in the charming work that followed a year later, *The Domestic Campaign*. In it he had assimilated the styles of Gluck, Mozart and Weber: there are more choruses, the choral writing has gained in assurance, and the melodies in appeal, while a considerably greater degree of skill is shown in the duos, trios and ensemble writing. The orchestral writing is impressive in its dramatic power and in Schubert's treatment of the brass, particularly with his liking for dark, mysterious trombone colouring, and in the horns, which he uses boldly and effectively, if not without echoes of Weber. Finally, Schubert had adopted the leit-motif, a development particularly noticeable in *Fierrabras*, though this did nothing to preclude further rejections at the Vienna Opera House.

The Kärnthnerthor Theatre.

Their good qualities notwithstanding, the majority of Schubert's operas were not mounted in his lifetime, a fact for which his preposterous libretti have not been unjustly blamed. The mounting of the absurdities of *Rosamunde*, the work of the fashionable bluestocking Helmine von Chézy, is quite inconceivable. This lady had made a name as the librettist of Weber's *Euryanthe*. Fortunately Schubert's collaboration with her as a popular author was not in vain in helping to establish his name in Vienna, for although the work collapsed after the tenth performance, the critics gave favourable notices to the entr'actes and the romance *The Moon shines over the peaks* and to the ballet music and choruses that still enchant us as they did all who heard them at the work's revival at the Salzburg Festival of 1937.

The only opera of Schubert's eligible for performance today is *The Domestic Campaign*. Castelli, its librettist, took his subject from Aristophanes, treating it as if the *Lysistrata* and *Women in Parliament* were re-written in accordance with the polite sentiment of the age of Biedermeier. Troubadour romance was all the rage, and accordingly a scenario of knightly chivalry was devised in a setting of conventional Middle Ages.

Castelli, proud of his book, which he at first entitled *Die Verschworenen* (*The Conspirators*), and was obliged by political considerations to change to *Der Häusliche Krieg*, published it in a collection of short dramatic pieces of 1823, remarking boastfully in the preface: 'Composers, you want good libretti, I have them.'

Schubert took up the challenge and set to work immediately upon the subject. In the Holy Land, knights are battling with the Saracens, while their ladies pine, believing themselves forsaken. The Countess of Lüdenstein invites to her castle the wives of those knights who are accompanying her husband on the crusade, and plots with them to prepare a grim welcome for their lords' return, a conspiracy which is joined by the Count's page Ugolin, who reveals it to his master, with various ensuing ramifications. The knights, apprised of the situation, parry their wives' indifference with unconcern, to the consternation of the anxious ladies who decide that as their masters are determined to return to the Holy Land, they will accompany them – and accordingly, they turn up in armour. The knights admit defeat, and all are reconciled, with the celebration of the nuptials of Ugolin amid general plaudits.

To this light-hearted libretto, Schubert wrote music no less pleasing, but of little originality. The choruses are reminiscent

Helmine von Chézy.

of *Freischütz*, which had been given the previous year in Vienna, the ariettas are Mozartian, particularly the romance 'Ich schleiche bang und still herum,' an almost literal quotation of Barbarina's aria at the beginning of *Figaro*, when she searches for the brooch that the Count has ordered her to take to Susanna.

In the principal scene, the conspiracy, which is full of life and humour, the leading soprano role is sung by the Countess, who is supported by a chorus of women, with string tremolandos and brass writing in which Schubert seems to be parodying grand opera; its counterpart is the scene in which the Count tells his knights of the ladies' plot, scored for bass solo and men's chorus, though without the subtlety of the ladies' scene. The reconciliation is based on a polonaise theme, and ends with a stately march heralded by the wind sections of the orchestra. Professor Einstein remarks perceptively of the scene in which the Countess in her aria replies to the Count, that Schubert is anticipating by some sixty years such operetta composers as Messager, since these two arias of his are as far removed from the classical aria as they are in advance of the fashionable romance of the 1820's. Both are light and elegant, and if a trifle facile, are never tasteless or banal.

But Schubert began to lose hope of hearing his new work performed, and abandoned it in favour of *Fierrabras* and *Rosamunde*, and it was not given till 1861, when it received a concert performance in Vienna on 1 March as an oratorio under the direction of Herbeck, and was later staged as an opera in August of that year in Frankfurt-am-Main. It was subsequently given in France, adapted by Wagner's translator Victor Wilder, under the title of *The Domestic Campaign*. In this age of festivals a good case could be made for its revival, with a production that might well afford to bring out the perhaps unconscious humour of the libretto, which is nevertheless so well underlined in the music.

Meanwhile, the work has been recorded by Viennese artists under the direction of Ferdinand Grossmann.

Thus, in 1823, already sick, and with few remaining illusions, Schubert was exhausting himself by composing three operettas in quick succession – only the last of them ever given, and for only

'The Domestic Campaign'.
Fresco at the Vienna Opera House by Moritz von Schwind.

two performances. He still clung to his ambition to write for the theatre, and not only for success, but as compensation for the realities of life. Unable to come to terms with them, he was forced to satisfy himself with dreams, and was tempted by the twofold theatrical illusion of comedy and emotion. The magic of the footlights is a powerful attraction to a nature as eager and vulnerable as Schubert's: in its essence illusion, yet one, in a sense, larger than life, since in order to move us on the stage, reality must be perfected, stripped and transformed by art.

Schubert's life was uneventful, without striking incident or the reckless adventures that inflame mind and sense; he needed the compensation of imagination. Out of this need sprang his great love of the poets, from whom he drew spiritual sustenance for his musical thought. They gave him the images, forms and adventures he lacked. He entered into their life and soul, and had the freedom of their domain. Herein lies the secret of his songs; for no self-engrossed composer could have had Schubert's close affinity with poets.

For the same reason he loved the theatre, finding in it the same escape as he found in poetry, an escape that was at times conscious and even deliberate, so anxious was he, as life had denied him the emotional experiences of actuality, to forget his sorrows in the world of fantasy. The libretti that seem so foolish to us may have appealed to Schubert for their very absurdity, in which he found charm, imagination and originality. Certainly, music, of its very nature, is fantasy, without the need of effort to make it so. 'Music', says Hoffmann, 'discloses to man unknown realms having nothing in common with the tangible world.' Schubert admired Hoffmann equally as writer and composer, particularly as the composer of *Undine*. He believed that music was of the essence of the world of the imagination; for even when music has a rapport with everyday life and known emotion, it is still compounded of sequences of sound – and of much else besides.

Schubert's escapism into a dream world was sometimes unconscious: it was at such times that he experienced the great moments of his artistic life. Theories have been put forward as to these times, of hallucination, schizophrenia, sleep-walking. He was possessed by another being, his familiar, both double and stranger. Spaun's description of the circumstances in which *Erlkönig* was composed leaves us in no doubt: we are admitted to the supreme moment, to the fire kindled by Goethe's poem, the transports and the tremendous birth-pangs of the song.

These were the processes of lyric creation, and Schubert was too innately lyrical to be a good theatre musician: therein lay the cause of his failure. For the theatre demands action, colour, observation: it is essentially an exteriorisation, whereas lyrical genius looks inwards, and it was from the depths of Schubert's spirit that his songs were begotten.

Schubert was rejected by the theatre; he failed where Mozart, with his boundless genius and worldly wisdom, succeeded. Schubert did not become disheartened until after the failure of *Rosamunde;* even so, he was noting down on his deathbed ideas for *The Count of Gleichen.* But it is evident that the year of 1823 sounded the knell of his hopes of success and fame. With the collapse of his enthusiasm for the stage, went also his will to conquer Vienna.

His failure in the theatre, with the threefold frustration of 1823, would not have been enough to dishearten Schubert, who was only twenty-six, with an ever-growing reputation, if sickness had not stricken him with despair. Syphilis, curable in our own time, was incurable in the nineteenth century. Schubert knew or at any rate suspected that he could not hope for a cure, and he sank into a nervous decline.

He saw his health ruined, his life wasted, the hopes of his youth brought to nothing. Something in him was shattered; the suggestion of hollow illusion present throughout all his work, now becomes a cry of anguish, heartbreak and unrelieved desolation. His sickness, associated with what the Church ordains as sin, may perhaps have appeared to him as the castigation for a dissolute life too given to wine and the pleasures of promiscuous love. His faith was too simple for him not to have discerned in his downfall the manifestation of divine wrath, a sign of the curse upon every man born into the world. In this agony he was horrified and bewildered, and on 8 May 1823 wrote down the *Prayer* in poetic form, in which he invokes the Almighty:

Tortured with holy grief, I yearn to live in a better world, and to fill this dark earth with a supreme vision of love.

Lord God, offer to Thy child, this child of misfortune, in token of redemption a ray of Thine eternal love.

Look on me, sunken in the mire, consumed by the fire of anguish. I go on my way in misery, and draw near to death.

Take my life, my flesh and my blood! Dip me in the waters of

'Imagination comes to console the poet'. Drawing by E. T. A. Hoffmann

Lethe, and deign, O Almighty One, to make of me a new man, stronger and more pure!

After having prayed God that he might die so that he might be reborn in a spiritual body, he nevertheless had recourse to human skill. His disease was treated with the remedies of the time, but they proved inadequate, and he had to spend some weeks in hospital, where he wrote part of *Die Schöne Müllerin*, and his great *Piano Sonata in A minor, Op. 143.*

On 30 November he writes to Schober:

I grieve at the state of our little circle as I do over all other eventualities, because, with the sole exception of my health, which, thank God, seems to have recovered, all goes very badly.

This hope of recovery proved vain. In December he lost his hair. Schwind writes to Schober 24 December:

'Schubert is better, it will not be long before he has his hair again, that had to be cut off because of his skin affection. He is wearing a most practical wig.'

It must have suited him ill. He was never really cured, and from this time on was a prey to nerves. He became full of self-doubt, and lost faith in the essential necessity of his work, and likely, also in his talent – as may be seen in his letter to Kupelwieser of 31 March 1824:

I feel I am the most miserable and unfortunate man in the world. Picture to yourself one whose health can never be re-established, who from sheer despair commits fault after fault, instead of amending his life. Picture to yourself a man whose high hopes are dead, to whom from henceforth love and friendship have nothing to offer but pain, who is even no longer aglow with the love of beauty – and tell me if that man is not for ever wretched . . . Each night when I go to sleep, I wish that I may never again awake, and each morning recalls the suffering of yesterday. So, joyless and friendless my days would pass if Schwind did not often look in . . .

Two weeks previously, he wrote in his note-book: *My works are the children of my musical wisdom and my suffering. That which pain alone begets is my last pleasure on this earth.*

He did not regain his self-possession until about 1826, when he had become resigned to his decline, going forth as if to meet his death, inscribing to it, as he opened his arms to it in welcome, his *D minor Quartet*. But he continued to suffer from severe headaches, and symptoms that were only too readily recognisable to him as those of venereal disease. When he fell victim to typhoid fever in November 1828, he had no resistance to offer save that of a weak and worn-out system.

(Moritz von Schwind.)

Lost Illusions

1824–1828

Once childhood and youth are left behind, nothing further happens that is capable of being a decisive force in shaping our nature and moulding our character: all has been said, particularly in the case of a talent so rare and so advanced, so resistant to other influences as was Schubert's. The remaining four years of his life held nothing new: the drama played itself out in the realm of his creative thought, the growth of his inner life. He was to accomplish the work he contemplated, but altered by sickness and the spectre of death, so that he became a stranger like the Wanderer on the face of the earth, the figure he had so often sung, in whom he saw what his own was to become.

Meanwhile, to all appearances his life continued in the same pattern, with forenoons of regular, productive work, desperate, at times frantic; afternoons of walks or visits, and evenings of the Schubertiads that in his sensitive, homeless life, took the place of home and children. He spent most of the year in Vienna. In the summer of 1824 he returned to Hungary, he travelled about the Tyrol with Vogl in 1825, and revisited his friends in Graz in 1827. Gradually his name became more widely known, his works were getting published. Life went on.

But the hidden rift widened from one year to another, and

Schubert composing.
(Lithograph by C. Bacchi.)

in spite of his insistence that he was cured, with which he tried to reassure his friends and himself, he knew it was but a stratagem. His manifold ailments, with the bad headaches that became ever more frequent, compelled his realisation: it was a slow decay. Thenceforth he was the prey of black moods, the dejection that never left him. Driven by his nervous state even more than by lack of funds, he constantly changed his lodgings, and drank increasingly to drown his misery.

He had to wage – against despair – the most exhausting struggle of all. Feeling himself to be marked out by death, he had to fence or come to terms with it in order to gain time in which to accomplish the work for which he was destined and which he had not yet completed. He had not yet written the sonatas and quartets he dreamed of, he had failed with his fourth symphony, – the *Tragic*, – had stopped mid-way in his eighth, the *Unfinished*. His powers had failed him. But he knew himself to be within sight of his objective, believing that he could carry the lied into the form of chamber music and symphony, and risking all in his efforts to prove it.

His only hope was to rally his powers, give up the theatre and all idea of worldly success, and turn his back on fame and fortune and his high hopes hitherto. It was necessary to sublimate them, weld them into a greater undertaking: that of the task to be finished, and the future. In Nietzsche's words, he must 'make out of deepest despair the most unconquerable hope', and aim at perfection within his soul. In this, Schubert perceived the significance of the issue: to count as good that which is propitious to the work of artistic creation, as harmful, all that is inimical to it.

His first need was for seclusion – not the grim seclusion forced upon Beethoven by his deafness, but a retreat within the world, compatible with Schubert's sociable, affectionate nature. During his working hours he was alone with his inspiration, on heights untrodden by others. He assumed a duality; and at these times, became most truly himself. His friends observed his dual personality, dumbfounded, admiring, and with some apprehension. 'Anyone who has seen him only once in the morning, in the throes of composition, his eyes shining, speaking, even, another language, will never forget it – though in the afternoon, to be sure, he became another person again...'

It mattered little to him that he was only one of his Emperor's humble subjects, unnoticed, neglected by his country, society and the world, so long as his solitary hours were free for the communion of the spirit; and found satisfaction in being of no account, so that he might dedicate himself completely to music.

He still cherished operatic projects from time to time, and in November 1828, ill as he was, he became engrossed once again in a libretto that his friend Bauernfeld had showed him the previous year, *The Count of Gleichen.* He dreamed of a brilliant score, and was gripped again by his passion for the theatre, and perhaps by the hope again of winning the elusive public. As he did so, he became delirious that very evening, and the following day he died.

He tried soliciting – without success – the posts of Kapellmeister to the Royal Chapel, and the directorship of the Kärntnerthor Theatre; but in spite of the opportunity they would have afforded him of getting performances of the works that he had never heard except in his head, how could a sick man, oppressed by loneliness and misgivings, have hoped to make a success of them? And yet it takes great strength of mind never to court official security, and Schubert was no stoic. Indeed, he would not have been Schubert if he had not had his vulnerable moments and had not continually surrendered himself to his illusory dreams. We find him the more lovable for his frailty. He was all too human... But fate stepped in and saw to it that he kept his resolution to renounce the world.

He soon found his decision justified, for he had the satisfaction of conspiring with the dark powers to produce, in January 1826, the *D minor Quartet*, *Death and the Maiden*, that he had begun two years previously. This time he triumphed over despair. The work that he had dashed down on to paper in 1824 as a challenge and token of victory, was now accomplished; and in the two remaining years this masterpiece was followed by yet others: the two *Piano Trios*, the *Impromptus*, the *Ninth Symphony*, the *Quintet in C*, *Die Winterreise*, *Nachtgesang im Walde* and the three last *Piano Sonatas.*

It was at this time that he found the solace of his second love. Schubert confided it to no one, and the woman he loved maintained a silence as discreet, so that no definite evidence has survived of this affair. But it seems likely that on the occasion of his second visit to the Esterhazys at Zelesz in summer 1824, he fell in love with Countess Caroline, and that she returned his affection. The memory of Theresa had dimmed – and how

Caroline Esterhazy in 1837. (Watercolour by Anton Hähnisch.)

changed he was since the days of his first love! All that in his relation with Theresa had been happy, light-hearted and frank, became in his feeling for Caroline, sad, sombre and anguished. This time there was no question of marriage and home, of a future as young lovers understand the word; the two found themselves faced with a hopeless love, never ultimately to be satisfied except in terms of eternity, to be consummated only by an act of faith. From Theresa, Schubert's love passed from an everyday level to an epic plane of spiritual marriage with Caroline, indissoluble, proof against all hazards, a pact in which only those united by it know whether they keep faith.

At all events, in 1828 Schubert dedicated to the Countess Caroline his beautiful *Fantasia in F minor, Op. 103*, for piano duet, with a devotion leaving no doubt as to his faithfulness, if he said, as he is reported to have said: *Are not all my works dedicated to her?*

Certain unions can only be ratified by silence. Schubert might have sung to his absent beloved the folk song:

> Wish me no welcome when I come,
> Bid me no farewell when I go,
> For when I come I never come
> And when I leave I never go.

Thus, on his return to Vienna at the end of October 1824, Schubert, at once radiant and anguished, lived in a kind of delirium. 'Schubert is back,' wrote Schwind to Schober on 8 November, 'well and divinely crazy, altogether rejuvenated by

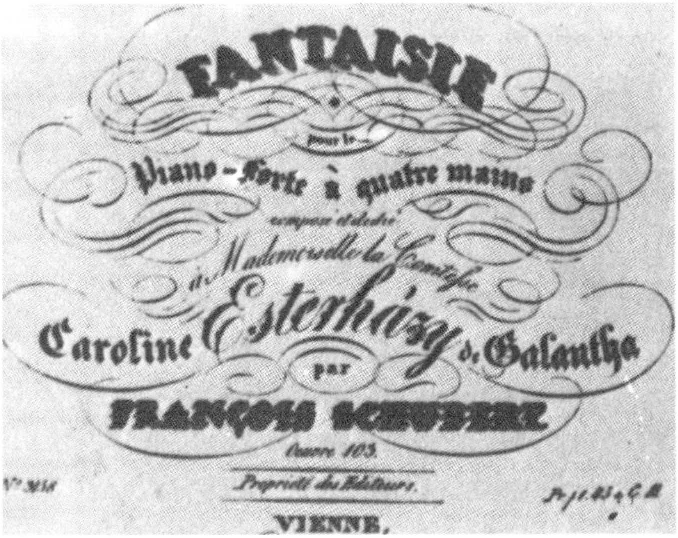

Title page of Fantasia, Op. 103, dedicated to Caroline Esterhazy.

joy, by pain, and by a carefree life' – a state he sought to prolong by the company of Moritz von Schwind, the painter he loved and cared for, in whose innocent youth he found comfort. And in 1825 there was a series of the most rapturously romantic Schubertiads, full of laughter and tears and imaginative fantasy. But by degrees sickness and dejection got the better of this self-confidence and assurance, and the bad days returned.

On 26 March 1827, Beethoven died. We do not know if Schubert ever saw the great veteran: Schubert's shyness as much as Beethoven's deafness and alarming temper could have constituted formidable obstacles. Nonetheless, Schubert venerated Beethoven as a giant, the very incarnation of music, with a timid adoration near to idolatry. He did not accompany his friends Hüttenbrenner and Teltscher when they visited the dying master, but in Bauernfeld's journal it is recorded that Schubert took part in the funeral on 29 March. *The Collector* of 14 April informs us that he was one of the thirty-six musicians who acted as torch-bearers on either side of the hearse. They were dressed in black and carried sprays of white lilies and roses bound with crape streamers, and held burning torches

Beethoven on his deathbed. (Drawing by J. Teltscher)

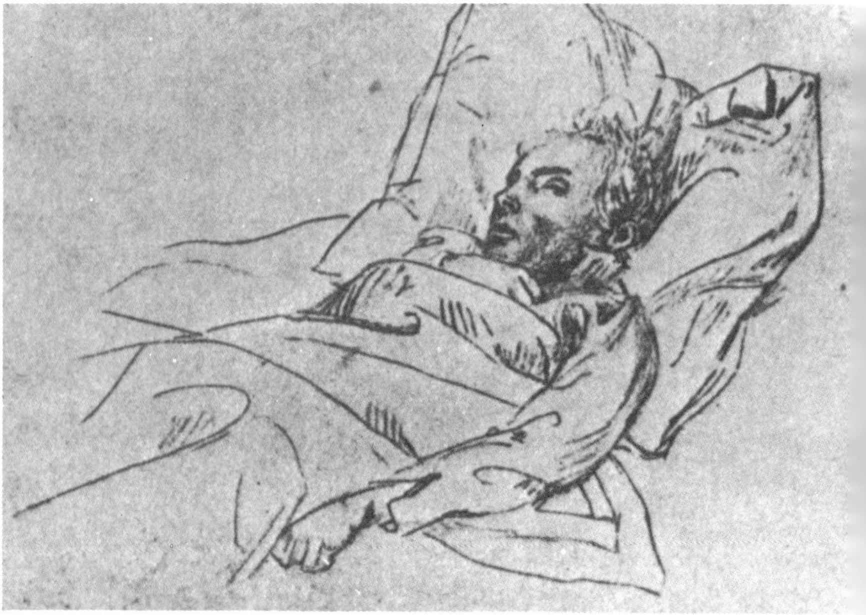

The Mehlgrüber Inn, visited by Schubert, Lachner and Randhartinger after Beethoven's funeral. Schubert drank to whichever of the three friends should die first (himself).

which they extinguished as the body was lowered into the grave. Grillparzer's funeral oration, which was read by an actor in the Währing cemetery, met with general approbation.

Schubert was distraught by Beethoven's death; it may have seemed to him the presage of his own. *Die Winterreise*, the twenty-four songs that comprise his most moving song cycle, begun in February and finished in October, was the more sombre and grief-stricken. To express his desolation, distress

(C. D. Friedrich, 1807.)

and premonitions of death, it was not to the olympian Goethe that Schubert turned, nor to Schiller, but to the kindly Müller, whose *Schöne Müllerin* he had already set, and whose grief echoed his own. The end of *The Winter Journey* is death. All acknowledge it, all leads to it, whether it is the grating *Weather*cock (No. 2) which announces that the wind has changed, *Irrlicht* (No. 9) (*The Will o' the Wisp*) of treacherous love, *The Crow* (No. 15) of sinister augury, or *The Sign Post* (No. 20) that guides the straying traveller back to the path – the path of death. Schubert broods on all that he has lost for ever, unclouded joys, innocent pleasures, gentle domestic things, and entitles his regrets *Der Lindenbaum* (*The Lime Tree*) (No. 5), *Backward Glances* (No. 8), *Frühlingstraum* (*Dream of Spring*) (No. 11). The leaves fall – *Letzte Hoffnung* (*The Last Hope*) (No. 16), – with the setting of the two suns that had illumined his life, and the amazing cycle ends with a picture of a wretched organ-grinder, jostled by the dogs, no hand outstretched to him – a too-convincing picture of the artist, as he works on amidst darkness, hostility and neglect.

The crushing grief expressed by the cycle, its desolation and sense of haunted solitude conveyed by superbly daring harmonic and rhythmic effects, the leaping intervals in the vocal line of *Letzte Hoffnung*, its portentous incantatory melodic invention, a sense of feverish hallucination plunged Schubert's friends into consternation and dismay; their genial Franz, good companion of the Schubertiads, the affable citizen, their easy-going, complaisant friend was no more to be found. They saw the terrible face of the angel in his hour of agony. They did not understand, nor would they understand, not from lack of love or from hardness of heart, but from the basic inability to communicate with another when that other lays bare his soul without thought of reserve – and it suffices to show one's heart to be thoroughly misunderstood.

Schubert had the pitiless experience of this on the autumn evening of 1827 when he sang *Die Winterreise* to his friends. Joseph von Spaun describes the occasion and the misconception

Manuscript of 'Frühlingstraum'.

that ensued. How alone Schubert must have felt in the midst of those he loved!

'Schubert was in a dark mood for some time; he seemed stricken. When I asked him what ailed him, he simply replied: *You will soon know and understand.* One day he said to me: *Come round to Schober's today, and I will sing you a cycle of lieder that will give you the shivers. I am curious to know what you will think of it. They cost me more than all my other lieder.* And he sang us, in a voice full of emotion, *Die Winterreise.* We were dumbfounded at the starkness of these songs, and Schober remarked at the end that only one of them had appealed to him, *Der Lindenbaum.* Schubert replied: *To me, these songs appeal more than all my others, and one day you will like them too.* He was right, for we were soon carried away by these sorrowful melodies that Vogl sang as no one else. I am sure that the feeling Schubert put into his most beautiful songs, and particularly into *Winterreise*, proclaimed his early death.'

Yet he had spent a delightful September at Graz, *the happiest days I have known for a long time*, he wrote in his letter of thanks to his hosts; but although joys came to brighten his existence, there was soon a return of the dejection and headaches that seemed to sound as a death knell. There was only one thing to do, compose, and compose so as to outstrip death. Before the end of 1827 he had written the *Piano Trio in E flat major* (*Op. 100*), the *Fantasy* (*Op. 159*) *for piano and violin*, and the *Four Impromptus* (*Op. 142*).

Early in 1828 he composed the *Fantasy in F minor* for piano, 4 hands, dedicated to Countess Caroline, *Miriams Siegesgesang* (*Miriam's Song of Triumph*), the *3 Klavierstücke*, and, most important, his '*Great*' *C major Symphony*, (*No. 9*). In June followed the *Mass in E flat major*, and that summer he wrote his *Quintet in C major* (*Op. 163*) for 2 violins, viola and 2 cellos, the three *Piano Sonatas* in A major, B flat major and C minor, and the fourteen songs that comprise the *Schwanengesang*. Who could survive such a prodigal expenditure of energy? It proved fatal as well as prescient, for Schubert died, having said all that he had to say.

At about this time, probably on his return from Graz, Schubert composed the *Six Moments Musicaux* (*Op. 94*), the pieces that are often reckoned as simple trifles, but that in reality, coming as they did at this troubled period of his life, are of

Huntsman in the Forest, by C. D. Friedrich, 1812.

much greater depth. In them, Schubert seems to be anticipating the mind of Musset, who was the first French poet to recognise his music. In his poem *Souvenir*, Musset exclaims:

> Dante, why do you say that there is no greater torment
> Than the memory of happiness in days of pain?
> What grief has inspired you with such bitter words,
> This affront to misfortune?

and he himself replies to his question:

> A happy memory on this earth, is
> Perhaps more real than happiness.

Schubert remembered his radiant visit to Graz during the difficult year of 1827, one that held also the happy memory of Zelesz in 1824. In the shrine and metamorphosis of memory, that fixes for ever the special quality of the remembered event, a bleak, oppressive present is of little account compared with the experienced moment of joy.

To meet his purpose he makes use of a piece that had previously appeared in *The Musical Album* of December 1823, under the title of *Russian Air*, and this he incorporated in a new set of four pieces, ending the set with a piece that had appeared in the same periodical in December 1825, under the title of *The Troubadour's Lament*. Whether or not Schubert intended the sequence as a suite in the classical sense, the first piece is in preludory style, the second, an andantino in A flat, is a mood of pathos, the third and best known of them all, the Russian tune, with its sprightly melody and left hand staccato accompaniment, is the 'happy memory' of Musset's lines. The fourth piece reflects the brilliant past and the barren present, the fifth flashes by in a challenging flurry of revolt, and the set ends with a return to the andantino's mood of shattered joy: Schubert's anguish, his diffidence and reserve. Like Mozart and Racine, he expresses himself with a restraint that is almost taciturn, a simplicity that confounds the philistine, pompous and crude.

Though the sequence may not be a suite, it has a decided poetic unity that compensates for the lack of the more formal attributes of the suite proper, a unity that is internal, existing

Schubert, by Moritz von Schwind.

in the relationship between the various numbers, which Schubert makes interdependent.

It was of the *Six Moments Musicaux*, the two sets of *Impromptus*, and the three *Klavierstücke*, a type of free piece with attributes of sonata form and scherzo devised by Schubert, and used after him by Schumann, Liszt and Chopin, that Schumann wrote: 'As a composer for the piano, he (Schubert) stands alone (in some respects even above Beethoven), in that his writing is more pianistic, that is to say, the piano's full resources are effectively brought into play, instead of as in Beethoven's piano writing, in which tone-colour has to be achieved more orchestrally, in terms of horn, oboe, etc. . . .' Schubert's lyrical power is evident without a poetic text to stimulate his imagination, and we are always impressed by it. In praising this quality, Schumann has also this to say of Schubert's music: 'He had the sensibility for the most subtle nuances, and gave to his music a diversity as great as the whole diversity of man.'

We wonder if those who were present on 26 March 1828 at the concert of Schubert's music given on the anniversary of Beethoven's death, shared Schumann's opinion?

The programme consisted of:

1. Movement from a new String Quartet (which, is not known).
2. Four Lieder: *Der Kreuzzug*, *Die Sterne*, *Fischerlied* (*Op. 96*), and setting of a fragment from Aeschylus, sung by Vogl.
3. *Ständchen* (*Op. 135*) (Grillparzer), version for soprano solo and women's chorus.
4. *Piano Trio in B flat* (*Op. 99*).
5. *Auf dem Wasser zu singen*, lied with horn and piano accompaniment.
6. *Die Allmacht*, sung by Vogl.
7. *Schlachtlied* (*Op. 151*), (Klopstock), for double male voice choir.

'Tremendous success, fine reception', wrote the generous Bauernfeld; but the critics remained cautious. Schubert, however,

Vogl and Schubert at the piano.
(Drawing by Moritz von Schwind.)

was untroubled by their censure and their grudging praise; he was busy scoring his '*Great C major*' *Symphony*.

The three last *Piano Sonatas* of September 1828 (in C minor, B flat major and A major) are a fresh landmark in Schubert's emancipation and lyrical mastery. Schumann perceives in them a certain resignation, as if with the approach of death, Schubert, burning with the desire to communicate his message once and for all, in his most essential and individual way, eschews brilliant pianistic effects in order to concentrate wholly upon poetical intensity. Thus, we find him hesitating, repeating himself, as we should linger with friends about to depart for a long time, and whom we may never see again – lingerings and prolixities for which he has often been criticised, and that are part of his adoration of music, his consideration for those who will love his music in time to come. He wants to bequeath to them now this, now that, wishing never to break his contact with the souls in sympathy, who sustain him in his earthly life, to whom will be committed his immortality. Schumann has felicitously remarked that this music, 'which seems as if it absolutely can not bring itself to come to an end, continues, ever tuneful and singing from page to page, interspersed here and there with more turbulent movements, but always soon lulled again.'

The first of the three sonatas, in C minor, the most Beethovenesque of all Schubert's sonatas, would seem, in its thematic conception and niceties of development, to be an offering of homage to the dead master. In its chromatic passages, the ascending semi-quaver figures like those of the *Pathéthique*, its alternating major and minor arpeggii, and spirited, strongly rhythmical finale, we are conscious of a heroic grandeur very distinctive from Schubert's intimate style. But in the *A major Sonata No. 20* that follows, there is a return – and particularly in the Scherzo and Finale in rondo form – to the veiled statements and heartfelt emotion that we have come to regard as especially Schubert's own.

But it is above all in his last sonata, *No. 21 in B flat major*, Schubert's musical last will and testament, that he reaches his supreme heights. For in the same way as he finally achieved in this year his ambition of magnifying the lied to a conception of symphonic dimensions in the '*Great C major*' *Symphony*, he made of his last sonata a sort of prolonged, unending lied, so long and varied and luxuriant, so personal and at the

The Shepherd on the Rocks. (anonymous print.)

same time so universal, that it seems to belong to eternity.

One is always tempted to take a composer's last work as final and conclusive – Schubert's swansong was, in fact, a lied: not one of those of the posthumous set of that name, but *The Shepherd on the Rocks*, with accompaniment for piano and clarinet or violoncello – but the sonata conveys so deep a longing, so agonising a grief, that it seems unmistakably to be Schubert's farewell to the world. As though with a premonition of his end, he has written mourning music. This *B flat major Sonata* is in classical form, but shows such freedom of expression in thematic interweaving, that Schubert seems to have emancipated himself from all bonds, and to be master of his art. The sonata is particularly characteristic in its exquisite treatment of modulation, its wealth of melody, and the special genius of outpoured tenderness and emotion which makes us believe that Schubert is speaking quietly, personally to each one of us.

In this year of 1828, he composed with an ardour and exuberance that resulted in undermining his already imperilled

health. In the words of Schumann, as he struggled with attacks of insanity: 'Compose, compose, so long as ever the day lasts...'

Exhausted, Schubert agreed to make a short journey with his brother Ferdinand and two friends to Eisenstadt, by way of a pilgrimage to the tomb of Haydn. His thoughts can only too well be imagined.

On his return he went to live with Ferdinand at Neue Wieden, in a house that was new and damp and aggravated his malady. From 13 October onwards he was unable to retain any food, and made a show of carrying on his life as usual. By the beginning of November, conscious that he had not the supreme mastery of form he admired in his hero Beethoven, he planned to make a further study of fugue and counterpoint with Simon Sechter, the Court Organist. But he had no time to take his first lesson.

The 12 November he writes to Schober: *I am ill. For eleven days now I have neither eaten nor drunk anything. I totter from the bed to the sofa and vice versa... If I swallow anything I promptly bring it up again.* On 16 November the doctors diagnosed abdominal typhus, caused by impure water. On 17th he was visited by Lachner and Bauernfeld, and discussed enthusiastically with them *The Count of Gleichen.* On the 18th he became delirious. According to Bauernfeld, he begged them not to leave him 'in that hole in the ground,' and when Ferdinand assured him that he was safely in bed at home, he cried: *No! it is not true. Beethoven is not lying here!*

He died on the morrow, 19 November 1828, at 3 o'clock in the afternoon.

All who attended his funeral in the Church of St. Josef in Margarethen on 21 November were affected by the grief of his family and friends. Schubert lay in his coffin dressed in a hermit's robe, a laurel wreath about his forehead. From the church, his body was taken to the Währing cemetery, at Ferdinand's instigation, in accordance with his undertaking to carry out Franz's wish to be buried close to Beethoven. Later, on the initiative of Grillparzer and Anna Fröhlich, a small monument was erected, designed by Schober in the form of a bust of Schubert in a niche between two columns. Grillparzer had it engraved with an inscription conspicuous more for affection than accuracy: 'Music has here interred a precious treasure and even fairer hopes.' It is true that Grillparzer left out of account Schubert's great works of his last two years,

The house where Schubert died.

'Christine at Schubert's tomb.'
(Illustration to a novel of 1836.)

his greatest claim to fame. Moritz von Schwind, delayed in Munich, writes to Schober a letter which shows him to have had a more intuitive realisation of Schubert's genius: 'I have mourned him as a brother, but now I rejoice for him that he passed in all his greatness and that his sufferings are at an end. The more I realise what he was, the more do I feel what he suffered.'

Thus, Beethoven and Schubert lay not far from one another at Währing until 1888, when the City of Vienna transferred them to the part of the Central Cemetery known as The Musicians' Pantheon, where the two rest even closer together.

Schubert's tomb. (lithograph, 1830).

The Lieder

It is not by chance that we have borrowed from Germany the word *lied.* We are familiar with popular song, romantic balladry, and art song. But lied describes a fusion so complete, so inherent in words and music, that there is no other term so apt. The secret of the lied's magic defies the words to which it is written; it is a universal spirit as well as the spirit of the countryside.

In its original usage the term signified all poetry that was declaimed or sung: in the Middle Ages as in remoter times, lyric poetry was first and foremost sung poetry. The lied is a brief communication, an expression of love, a swift outpouring of emotion. Since the Middle Ages, it has continued to well forth in its dual capacity, popular and scholarly.

After the sober interlude of the Reformation, the intellectualism of the Age of Enlightenment which preferred the more baroque form of the cantata and the aria, the lied flowed afresh when German youth re-formed itself upon medieval tradition, and, led by Herder, Goethe and Schiller, took to singing the love of nature and freedom.

Thus, in order that the lied as we know it might be brought

Sepia by Moritz von Schwind for the ballad 'Der Liedler' .1822.

to birth, it was necessary to await romanticism's return to source, its revival of national consciousness, and taste for folklore and local tradition. The world had to await Schubert, the most poetic, as Liszt said, of all composers, that is to say, one who was also a poet whose native tongue was music. To say that he was possessed by poetry would still be inadequate – for he was one with it.

He is regarded as the lied's creator, though since the latter half of the eighteenth century many composers have written songs of popular appeal, not forgetting the poets Reichardt, Zelter, Steffan, Zumsteeg, whose ballads Schubert at first imitated; as well as Haydn, Mozart (with special reference to *Abendempfindung an Laura, K 523*) and also Beethoven. But Schubert, by his adoption of the rhythm of the spoken word, was the first to transmute poetry and the natural tones of the voice into song, and to enshrine in poetry and music the common spirit of humanity.

The very term lied is sufficient to conjure up the spirit of romance, the lifting of heart, the immeasurable longings, the emotional ferment and spirit of revolt – all our inner turmoil that releases the springs of poetry and song. In the face of jejune romances, the refinement, confined to a polished minority, of French song, the lied presents its sturdy growth, its warmth and freedom, and its particular genius in which it is at one with the soul of a people, a nation's character.

Schubert's lieder are the chief foundation of his work: the point of departure, the point of return, if we are to penetrate to the heart of his music, to discern the artist's underlying design, his original purpose, and his greatest claim to fame, which lies in his infusion of the lied's lyricism into every branch of music, his achievement in extending it into terms of chamber music and symphony. Out of an originally short and popular composition, Schubert created one of the finest, most productive forms of romanticism.

His mastery of the lied is undisputed; but his achievement does not rest at that, nor must we limit ourselves to it in our assessment of him as did Grillparzer and some of his friends, as did the nineteenth century, and as some still do today. Schubert's greatness is rooted in the lied, it is not contained by it.

It is not feasible to base one's appraisal of Schubert's songs on their chronology, their subject matter or style: each should

Heidenröslein
(Engraving by W. von Kaulbach.)

be considered on its own; they vary only in the degree of their inspiration that flows as freely and spontaneously as folk song, with which they have a delicate affinity. Schubert had no hesitation about rewriting any composition with which he was not satisfied: there are four and five versions of particularly difficult poems by Goethe. His inspiration, if it was not subjected to control in its earliest stages, was subsequently appraised with a critical eye. He had no easy complacency about his works, and distinguished sharply between excellence and perfection. In his lieder we find the finest alongside the less successful, though the latter would make many a composer's fortune.

It is likewise impossible to find a development or change of style; ever since 1814 with *Gretchen am Spinnrade*, Schubert had found an individual utterance, a personal style. Subsequently he was to do other things, but he never did anything better. His earliest works have the same bold harmonic treatment, the same animation as *Winterreise* and *Schwanengesang:* his songs reflect all the emotions of his guileless, sensitive nature; therein lies the secret of their elusive charm, their most abiding beauty. The most appealing are those that retain the spontaneity of the traditional folk-verses they so nearly resemble, as *Im Frühling*, *Auf dem Wasser zu Singen*, *Die Forelle* or *Heidenröslein;* but he is also as capable of the tragic power of *Erlkönig*, *Die Junge Nonne*, and *Der Doppelgänger*, as of touching the heights of the symbolist, supernatural poetry of *Prometheus* and Goethe's *Ganymed.* Lightheartedness, gaiety and the joy of living alternate with melancholy, desolation and the corroding doubts of a nervous condition, both aspects shown in the duality of mood of *Die Schöne Müllerin.*

Whatever he has to say he always says naturally and aptly, unforced in manner and feeling. He is adept at combining dramatic power with simplicity: there is no clamour, no overemphasis, none of the romantic bombast that at times ensnares Schumann. Even in *Winterreise* he does not seek to dramatise, although the poems' subject and treatment, and his own personal circumstances offered him every inducement to do so.

In all his music he maintains restraint and a 'sweet reasonableness'; he suggests suffering rather than conveys it, his smile is always a trifle inscrutable. Schubert expresses the essential enigma of our human nature and state, an ambiguity not to be conveyed by shouting, clamour and gesticulation or dogmatic assertion. The search for truth begins with self-searching, and

Die Schöne Müllerin
(Engraving by B. Brend'Amour.)

Schubert pursues it always scrupulously and ardently, with discretion and a sense of mysticism, as a solitary who seeks artistic revelation no less than the soul's perfection. It involved a battle won on a spiritual and personal plane; because of it, after Schubert had tried in vain to storm the gates of the theatre and conquer the social world, he returned to lieder to achieve the consummation of his art, to express his dreams and emotions in a style in which he has remained unrivalled: a lyrical power that requires both the conquest of self and its identification with the spirit of mankind. It is this which gives his songs their emotional force and their ultimate beauty, unique to Schubert.

The contrast between the simple, flowing melodic line and the complexity of the accompaniment reveals clearly the dual strain in Schubert's character. The accompaniment sometimes becomes almost independent, having always a strongly marked individuality; Schubert conceives it symbolically, giving it a role of equal importance with the voice, treating it sometimes decoratively, as in *The Trout*, sometimes as abstract (*Die Junge Nonne*), more often both at once – *Erlkönig*, *Doppelgänger*, *Winterreise*. His harmonic scheme is one of striking simplicity of means, and entirely personal to himself. His modesty and restraint are apparent in the spread chords: substitute for these the heavier treatment of Schumann's lieder, and the mood is altogether different, the effect defeats itself, and the music loses its most moving quality. His apparent awkwardnesses, the ingenuousness of his varying moods, castigated by the critical sages of the nineteenth century, ascribed by them to ignorance, the daring, piquant individuality of his harmonies so much admired by Ravel, the faculty he shared with Mozart of being able to create an atmosphere by altering one note – a change unexpected yet somehow anticipated – and finally a remarkable economy of means, these are what give Schubert's lieder their expressive power and individual beauty.

Schubert and Goethe

It has been said that in his choice of poets Schubert failed to discriminate between the best and the worst: beside Goethe, Schiller, Heine we find Rellstab, Leitner, Matthisson; and as well as his friends Mayrhofer and Schober, in whose favour he was biased by his affection for them, what a collection of indifferent writers there was, who failed to achieve even their moment of fame in the 1820's! But is *The Trout* less sparkling because of Schubart's words, and *Nachtgesang im Walde* any the less romantic for having been inspired by Seidl? In his interpretation of Goethe, Schubert is too sensitively discriminat-

Goethe's Lieder, dedicated to Goethe.

ing to leave us in any doubt as to his literary and poetic perception: he made several versions of extracts from Goethe's *Wilhelm Meister* (*Wer sich der Einsamkeit ergibt*), of which there is one of November 1815 and three of autumn 1822; and five attempts at *Mignon's Song* (*Nur wer die Sehnsucht kennt*). Between 1816 and 1821, Schubert resumed five times his setting of the fine *Gesang der Geister über den Wassern* that Goethe wrote in 1779 on his travels in the Bernese Oberland, inspired by the Staubbach waterfall near Lauterbrunnen. The torrent falls in a single cascade of some three hundred metres into the depths of the gorge, where it is lost in whirlpools and showers of spray. Scene, spirit and imagination are possessed by such elemental force, and to it we owe the poem of inspired mystical pantheism that was the last of Goethe's 'Sturm und Drang' period.

Schubert's fifth version (February 1821) for eight male voices and string orchestra, catches so minutely the subtlest nuances of the poem that this example alone will serve to show his realisation of the respective merits of the texts he chose, just as the substantial list of lieder of which he gives two versions refutes the legend of Schubert as incompetent to criticise and amend, producing the final draft at once. Although *Erlkönig* and *Gretchen am Spinnrade* came into being with such lightning rapidity, others among his greatest works, such as the fifth version of *Gesang der Geister*, were far from being the fruits of a single stroke of inspiration.

Schubert had a passionate admiration for Schiller, then Goethe. His displeasure with the Sage of Weimar did nothing to damp the ardour of his veneration: to him, Goethe was always the supreme poet. In his settings of such poems as *Wanderers Nachtlied* and *Über allen Gipfeln ist Ruhe* – which contains infinity in two lines – he was attempting to transmute into music what was essentially elusive. Did he succeed? At all events, his temerity bears witness to his love of Goethe.

No more fortunate in his literary enthusiasms than in his human affections, he received no response from Goethe, and it is interesting to speculate as to the reason why he did not manage to attract the respect of his contemporary, or even his attention.

In April 1816, Spaun felt it was an auspicious moment to send Schubert's lieder to Goethe, forty-four of whose poems had already been set by the nineteen-year-old composer, including *Erlkönig*, *Gretchen am Spinnrade*, *Trost in Thränen*, *Schäfers Klagelied*, *Sehnsucht*, *Meeresstille*. Spaun enclosed with the songs a letter to His Excellency, asking permission for Schubert to dedicate *Erlkönig* to him. It is a matter for speculation whether the letter even reached Goethe. He received so many every day that his secretaries had to sift them out and the good-hearted Spaun's strong and formal request was probably cast aside, for it remained unanswered, and the approach in vain. In such matters Goethe consulted his colleague Zelter, who composed music himself and was extremely classical-minded; he was making settings of the Master's poems, so that one can imagine what he must have thought about Schubert.

Gesang der Geister über den Wassern.
(Wilbad Gastein, anonymous print.)

Could Bettina have been thinking of Zelter when she attacks the academics in a letter of Christmas 1810? 'Inner ferment and the unconscious, which in all art and science are the well-spring of genius, have reached in music their highest degree; and no one will plumb these depths. We are forever dogged by the shattering mediocrity of the academic.'

Poor Franz did not stop to reflect that Goethe had not even troubled to read the letter, he felt himself snubbed by the great poet who was his hero, a betrayal which hurt him considerably.

Goethe has often been reproached for his failure to understand the romantics: Hölderlin, Beethoven, Weber, Kleist did not find favour in his eyes. Goethe saw in them all that he most hated in the world, sickness, chaos, extravagance and folly. His godlike mind was confronted with a rebuttal in the face of these pathetic geniuses: it seemed as if Apollo were denying existence to Dionysus. Goethe felt that the very roots of his being and fame were in jeopardy. He was no saint: he brushed away the intruders with a wave of his hand.

Schubert's case was different. No other composer has set Goethe's poetry with such fidelity, sensitivity and felicity: an identification of composer with poet that would seem to be a case of second sight and demonic possession.

Romain Rolland has finely analysed the nature of Goethe's reactions to music (Goethe and Beethoven, Chap. IV). As Goethe misjudged Beethoven and Schubert, one concludes that he lacked understanding of music – yet he possessed a sound musical education in singing, piano and violoncello. He could read a simple score and judge the quality of a work; but his taste remained that of the eighteenth century, and his god, Mozart. His lifelong regret was that Mozart should not have set his *Faust* to music. What a sequel it would have made to *Don Giovanni*!

Goethe demanded inspiration of music ('I can always work better when I have been listening to music', 1820); he required it to be soothing and intellectually stimulating. He hated noise, passion, all that stirs mind and heart. Romantic music aroused in him only suspicion: he was shocked and repelled by it, and one suspects Zelter's reactions to have been similar.

To Goethe, who was more of a visual artist than a musician,

Zum sehen geboren,
Zum schauen bestellt
(Born to see,
Doomed to look)

words were of chief importance: the poem was self-sufficient; neither music nor illustration could illumine where words had failed.

In 1816, Schubert was unknown: Goethe must have thrown away both Spaun's letter and the collection of lieder, even supposing that they had reached his hands. But on 16 June 1825, Goethe received with a quartet by Mendelssohn, three of Schubert's finest Goethe settings: *An Schwager Kronos* (1816), *Mignon* (1815) and *Ganymed* (1817). He thanked Mendelssohn, with whom he was personally acquainted, and whose limited taste he admired; but there was not a word for Schubert, although when Wilhelmine Schröder-Devrient sang *Erlkönig* to him in his home in 1830, he was full of admiration. How was it that he had been mistaken?

The poet had conceived something simple and rural, in folk song style, and the composer had made of his unpretentious legend a nightmare drama, had turned his classically ordered poem into a romantic confusion of tempest, thunder and lightning. Goethe's displeasure is imaginable at finding his rightful *Erl King* unrecognisable in this metamorphosis of genius. It was foreign to him; he deemed his poem not transfigured but disfigured. In 1830 his attitude was changed by an inspired performance that opened his eyes and ears. He paid tribute to the memory of Schubert, and kissed the brow of the singer who had sung the song so well.

Thus this man of 80 was able to experience the new music: it was something of a marvel. 'This din exhausts me', he remarked in conversation of the orchestration of Spontini's *Vestal Virgin*. 'There must be a limit which one cannot overstep without the ear's rebellion'.

In this 'limit' we recognise the classicist, the conception of proper limits, rational frontiers. Molière's lines come to mind:

Men, for the most part, are strangely made.
In real nature they are never found.

Wilhelmine Schröder-Devrient.

The romantic aims at the infinite, and because of it, strives always to defer the limit he instinctively repudiates.

Goethe was impervious to Schubert's musical expression of his poems. He fashioned a magic world that inspired Beethoven, Schubert and Weber, though he himself did not enter into the composers' works inspired by his poems. For poetry has its own music, and a poet will always prefer it to composers' music.

Goethe wrote to Humboldt on 3 December 1808: 'Music is purely irrational, and speech has only to do with reason', a saying paraphrased by Bettina in a letter to Goethe, (1810): 'All want to express themselves rationally in music; and the true nature of music is precisely that it begins where reason leaves off.'

Bettina pleads the cause of the irrational: one imagines that she might have appealed to the surréalists, and that André Breton might have called her 'The girl with the dynamic imagination.' She had an instinctive love of Schubert. Her visits to Beethoven gave her a liking for this music that was freed from cerebral technicalities, where instinct was allowed free range, and the ideal of the individual, of the individual spirit, was accepted as of the deepest significance.

Liedertafel

Schubert had many rivals in the nineteenth century, but even Schumann and Brahms, who came nearest to his genius, did not surpass him. Nowhere is greater purity of shape, clarity of expression or surer melodic instinct. Schubert had a kind of extrasensory perception: with him it was as if the lied were a direct emanation of his subconscious.

He excelled not only in songs for one voice, but also in choral writing for various voices – vocal quartet, double quartet, male voice quartet, and choral writing on a more important scale. This type of collective lied was still, in accordance with the basic Germanic community instinct, a matter of personal inspiration, the expression of personal emotions within the group. Schubert brought it to perfection.

At the beginning of the nineteenth century, associations of amateur male singers were formed in Germany, the first of

A rehearsal at Lachner's. (Drawing by Moritz von Schwind.) →

them being founded by Zelter, Goethe's musical adviser; and soon there was not a town or village of the German-speaking countries that had not its *Liedertafel* or local male-voice choral society, the equivalent of the *Orphéons* in France and the *Glee Clubs* in England. Their success was immediate, and the movement spread rapidly. As it was an amateur cult, the composer had to be simple and practical, and Schubert produced in this medium works widely varied in form, choral lay-out and accompaniment, some unaccompanied, the majority with piano accompaniment. The two finest are scored for other instruments: *Nachtgesang im Walde* (*Op. 139b*, *1827*), for two tenors and two basses, with four horns, mostly in unison, playing antiphonally with the voices, suggesting the spell of the forest at night; and *Gesang der Geister über den Wassern*, the fifth and best version of which dates from February 1821, laid out for four tenors and four basses with an accompaniment of two violas, two cellos and double bass.

No one, since the Italian madrigal, had written such music; but Schubert formulated his not on Monteverdi or Luca di Marenzio, but rather on the singing of his friends in the Schubertiads, or the peasants in the villages of his walks in the Viennese countryside. He insisted on being true to his own idiom.

In this context should be mentioned also a fascinating chorus for women's voices written in July 1827, a few months after *Nachtgesang im Walde:* the *Serenade*, setting of words by Grillparzer, '*Zögernd leise*'. Anna Fröhlich had asked Schubert to write her a song for the birthday of one of her pupils. Accordingly, he wrote her first of all a setting for mezzo soprano solo with accompaniment of male voice quartet. But Anna demanded a chorus for women's voices; her wish was gratified, and to it, we owe in the sad year of 1827, one of Schubert's most melting and pellucid works. It was performed on 11 August on a beautiful night, in Joseph von Lang's garden at Döbling, the refrain of 'stille, leise' suggestive of the sound of the wind in the branches, lending an enchanted and somewhat poignant atmosphere to this happy music, as if the young girls in the choir were touched with the sense of the evanescence of human joy.

Variations on his own style

Schubert makes use several times of his lieder in his chamber music. The second movement of the *D minor Quartet* consists of a set of variations on *Death and the Maiden*, the fourth movement of his *Quintet in A major*, of variations on *The Trout*. *Trockne Blumen* (*Faded Flowers*), the eighteenth song in the *Schöne Müllerin* cycle, forms the basis of the *Introduction and Variations in E minor for Flute and piano* (*Op. 160*). In the theme of the third movement of the *Fantasy Sonata in C major for Violin and Piano* (*Op. 159*) we find *Sei mir Gegrüsst*. Finally, the four movements of the *Wanderer Fantasy* have their germ in the central idea of *Der Wanderer* (published 1821), which provides the theme of the variations of the Adagio. Musicologists have been struck with this propensity of Schubert's, and have remarked that it is rare to find a composer borrowing from his own material, citing as their only instance the case of Haydn and the '*Emperor*' *Quartet*. Some of Schubert's commentators see in this singularity of his only an over-fondness for his own works, an artistic narcissism scarcely in accordance with Schubert's character. Professor Deutsch more justifiably thinks that 'a particularly satisfactory song demanded of Schubert instrumental expression also', though considering Schubert's large-scale project for the lied, it seems as if the five instances of his use of it in his chamber music must have been experiments he made in the process – experiments that helped him to know that his project could be realised, and that one day all his music, on however grand a scale, would be as a song straight from his heart, the lyrical expression so essentially of the lied.

The *Wanderer Fantasy* of November 1822, written immediately after he had abandoned the *Unfinished Symphony*, was published by Cappi and Diabelli in 1823, and is one of the strongest, most original of Schubert's piano works. A stumbling block to the majority of pianists on account of its formidable technical demands, it is rarely enough included in piano recitals: yet though of a brilliance not found in Schubert's more intimate works, it is not merely a set of pianistic formuli, for Schubert is again creating his own characteristic utterance, in which its problems in performance are inherent.

This 'Fantasy' in the German sense of poetic imagination, the free play of creative fancy, a reverie in sound, is in four movements in free sonata form. In structure it is classical: an Allegro with two subjects, Andante and Variations, Presto in the form of Scherzo, and concluding Fugue. Its originality lies in the interweaving of these four movements, and their unification in the single lied theme of *The Wanderer*. Schubert's particular achievement in 1822 was in having attained to this unity for which he was striving. Imbued with his desire for it, seeking to reconcile every element in a basic lyricism, he makes of the Adagio the central feature of the work, from which radiates its whole meaning and colour. All is disposed around the lied.

The Allegro opens with cumulative chords that suggest the idea of personal tragedy and a state of deep perturbation: a sombre statement of the principal idea: 'I am everywhere a wanderer'. The chromatic surge of the first movement initiates and balances the troubled first theme, and is still present with the second, which is gentler and more soothing, and introduces the Wanderer theme ('O Land where art thou that I call my own?') And in the variations we have no perfunctory exercise on the tune, but the shifting expression of Schubert's mood of nostalgic longing.

The delicious Scherzo, all lightness and poetry, a fleeting smile in a tragic world, recalls the Wanderer's days of happiness in his lost homeland, with a resemblance to the lied which Schubert composed a few weeks later, in December 1822, to Goethe's poem *Der Musensohn*. Beneath a deceptive simplicity, seeming to be quite unaware, Schubert produces here a masterpiece of artless ingenuity.

The final Allegro resumes the two contrasting themes of the initial Allegro, combining them in fugal form, a treatment so convincingly natural that one is scarcely conscious of its more academic implications. It bears out the song's last phrase: 'There where thou art not, there is happiness.'

We can see how Schubert seeks to give unity to the separate movements of the classical sonata, which had often no other link than in their tonality. His approach is that of a poet. He takes a central idea of both musical and emotional significance, developing it in terms of poetry and music in the light of his candid, ordered, natural lyricism, a poesy that could smile through tears and still cherish a hidden sorrow in the midst of unalloyed gaiety.

The Chamber Music

From his youth Franz played chamber music; the Schubert family were his example. As soon as he was able, he took part in the family quartet with his father and elder brothers, as a viola player, like Bach, Mozart and Beethoven.

The first seven string quartets written at the Convict 1812–1814, and collected in the Breitkopf Complete Edition under the title of Series V, are written in classical style, with the exception of the first, which has five movements and some remarkable key-changes, opening with an introduction in C minor, D minor, and G minor, in spite of the fact that the main part of the work is in B flat major. The first movement, Andante, which opens in G minor, has extended passages in D major and D minor; the other movements are in F and B flat major. Since his youth, Schubert was a good enough student to know when he was being unorthodox; if he broke the rules it was because he was already venturing upon the harmonic experiments which he was to make again in his last works, this time at the height of his powers. In his first quartet he emancipates himself from the classical form to which he defers in his other early quartets, and in which he contrives to establish his individuality from the outset. The others are the achievement

Trio Sonata (anonymous painting.)

of an exceptionally-gifted disciple of Haydn and Mozart. His borrowings from the classical masters apply to their symphonic works, a fact doubtless to be accounted for by his performances in the works played by the Convict orchestra: we catch an echo of Mozart's *Symphony in C major* (*K 338*) in the *Second Quartet*, of the *G minor Symphony* in the Minuet of the *Ninth Quartet*, and of Beethoven's *Second Symphony* in the Minuet of Schubert's *Seventh Quartet*.

In these youthful essays it is possible to follow Franz's progress in the development of themes and in formal structure. Whatever has been said on the subject, he attached great importance to technique, and determined to master it; and although later on he appeared to relegate it to a secondary position, it was because he had discovered other priorities for his attention.

The *Eighth Quartet in B flat major* (1814) already sounds distinctly Schubertian; but we have to wait for the *Quartet Movement* (*Quartettsatz*) *in C minor* (the original Allegro movement of an unfinished quartet of which only a few bars of the Andante remain), to find the Schubert we love. The atmosphere of this tragic, passionate work recalls that of *Erlkönig*. Its structure is that of sonata form; its tonality is so unexpectedly varied, so attractive and colourful that we recognise immediately the unmistakable stamp of Schubert.

The disparity indicative of a distinct change of idea, between Schubert's *Eleventh* and *Twelfth Quartets*, has often been compared with that between Beethoven's *Quartet in E flat major* (*Op. 74*) and his *Quartet in F minor* (*Op. 95*). Schubert was finding his own personal idiom at only twenty-three years of age.

The *Thirteenth Quartet in A minor* (*Op. 29, No. 1*), his only one in this key, and the only one to be published in his lifetime, emphasises the characteristics of his newly-discovered form of expression. It was written in February or March 1824, when Schubert had succeeded in overcoming the despair into which his illness had plunged him. In a letter of 31 March to Kupelwieser who was in Rome, Schubert expresses his sorrow and perturbation by quoting Gretchen's song: 'Meine Ruh ist hin, mein Herz ist schwer, Ich finde sie nimmer und nimmer mehr!' ('My peace is gone, my heart is sore, I find it never and never more!') – and he adds *This is what I should be singing every day, for every night when I go to sleep, I wish never to wake again...*

Was it consciously that at this date he removes all barriers between the lied and chamber music, in his desire to treat instrumental music as lied on a bigger scale? Or is he influenced by his recollection of his famous song? However this may be, there is a reference to *Gretchen am Spinnrade* in the opening bars of the *Thirteenth Quartet*.

The Andante seems to relax into a tender smile, one of its themes borrowed from the third entr'acte of *Rosamunde*, and the Minuet's Trio opens with an exact quotation from a lied composed in 1820 to a poem by Schiller, *Götter Griechenlands* (*The Gods of Greece*) – 'Schöne Welt, wo bist Du?' – regret for a fallen world conceived as the pattern of beauty and virtue. Perhaps Schubert is thinking of his youth, which seems to him as remote and inaccessible as Sophocles' Greece. The mood of longing that fills him is contrasted with the mazurka rhythm

Head of a Girl, by Friedrich Wassmann.

of the Minuet, giving it its bittersweet poignancy, subtle and profoundly piteous. The finale, based on martial Hungarian themes, tries vainly to recapture the eagerness and untroubled gaiety of old. Schubert has entered upon a new period of his existence. His friends are aware of it; Schwind writes, after the concert of 14 May 1824 at which the quartet received its first performance by Schuppanzigh's quartet: 'Schubert's quartet was performed, rather slowly in my opinion, but with great clarity and delicacy. Its total effect is very moving, as, like the lieder, it leaves one with melody, and is all feeling and significance. The work had a great ovation, particularly the Minuet, which is of remarkable refinement and purity.'

All that Schubert had discovered by the beginning of 1824, that he had found by searching, experimenting, was brought to its consummation in the *Fourteenth* and *Fifteenth Quartets* of 1826. This time he wrote two masterpieces known to all the world, the first, the *D minor Quartet, Death and the Maiden,* in which the quartet is almost overwhelmed by the work's emotional vehemence and the ascendancy of the lied; the last in *G major* (*Op. 161*), which, in its perpetual vacillation between major and minor, and its unusual key-changes, is typically Schubertian.

The opening Allegro of the D minor quartet seems to be asking an urgent question, which is answered by a simple, serene Andante, as artless as a folk song.

The Scherzo and Trio are in contrast with the furious finale, arresting in its dynamic rhythms and stark harmonies. Schubert makes use of dissonances, tonal clashes, abrupt transitions from one key to another in his effort to express his agitation and dismay. He has achieved the utmost freedom of expression. Already the quartet had ceased to be for him a classical medium devised for the mind's pleasure and the ear's enchantment, in which slow movements alternate with quick, sad with lively, sprightly and gay: it became now a lyric utterance, a prolonged colloquy, the laying bare of his heart.

Already in his *Octet* of 1824, he had aimed at giving to a work of apparently classical form a significance very different from that of his model, Beethoven's *Septet*. The resemblances between the two works would seem to indicate that Schubert was intentionally emulating the master: the work is similarly planned in six sections (though in the *Octet* the Minuet and Scherzo are in inverse order), with the same instrumental lay-out for clarinet, bassoon, horn, violin, viola, cello, and bass (though the *Octet* has two violins). The work was first performed in the spring of 1824 at the house of Count Ferdinand Troyer, the amateur clarinettist who commissioned it, and has always been highly esteemed among Schubert's works for its strength, its happy serene atmosphere, the charm of its two Andantes, and the spaciousness of its design, always full of interest and variety. The theme of the fourth movement variations is taken from the love duet of Schubert's youthful operetta *Die Beiden Freunde von Salamanka* (1815): the first variation for solo violin, the second for clarinet and bassoon, the third for horn, the fourth for cello, and the two last for full ensemble, a scheme that saves the work from meretricious virtuosity and allows Schubert scope for highly original treatment. There is a link between the anguished opening of the finale and the *Thirteenth Quartet*, which was written about the same time; otherwise the work is mainly cheerful in character.

Similar characteristics are to be found in the two *Piano Trios* (in *B flat major, Op. 99*, and in *E flat major Op. 100*), probably both of 1827, so popular with amateur chamber players. Schubert does not assume the attitude of inspiration in communicating his thoughts to us, he whispers them with persuasive charm, so naturally and unaffectedly that at first one is scarcely aware of his mastery. The *Trio in B flat* is, if anything, overshadowed by the *E flat Trio* that followed, with its first movement theme of matchless beauty, its apparently inexhaustible resources and organic growth.

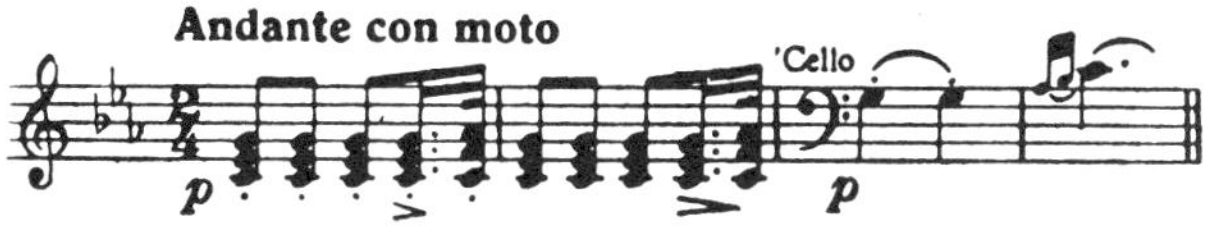

Moods and passages have the ease and charming unexpectedness that are always recognisably Schubert's. The second movement, based on a Swedish folk melody, *Se Solen sjunker* (*See, the sun goes down*), is striking in its poetic nordic atmosphere. The finale, unusually designed as scherzo, trio and allegro, is a triumph of design – for to Schubert, freshness and originality of form, as well as the actual content of the music, are the means whereby he communicates the message close to his heart.

The *Trio in E flat* was performed 26 December 1827 at the Vienna Music Club, and again at Schuppanzigh's in the following January. In a letter to Hüttenbrenner of 18 January 1828, Schubert says that *everyone liked it very much. Bocklet, Schuppanzigh and Linke played it splendidly*, – a remark typical of Schubert's modesty. From its very first bars, with their suggestion of the posthorn's call, this trio enchants and transports us, and does not relinquish its hold until its final conclusion. In the idyllic Andante we wander in the Viennese woods and fields. The Scherzo is fantasy – a fantasy of humour and childish mischief. The Rondo is a movement of sheer fun, the joyous, direct. sane music of a man sick and without hope. The artist's work remains impassive in the face of the tears with which it was brought to birth.

With his special musical insight and his devotion to Schubert's music, Schumann wrote in 1838 of the *Trio in E flat:* 'It is about ten years since a trio by Schubert passed, like the portent of a stormy sky, over the disturbances of the contemporary musical scene.' He finds this trio 'more stirring, virile and dramatic' than the *Trio in B flat*, and sees in the opening Allegro 'a deep indignation and a limitless nostalgia'. In the Andante, he says, are 'sighs that would rise and spread until they swell into the heart's anguish', and in his opinion, Schubert is at his finest in the finale.

In August-September 1828, six months after the *'Great C major' Symphony*, followed the *Quintet in C major (Op. 163)*, for 2 violins, viola and 2 cellos. As it was not published until 1853, Schumann may not have known it. The two *Piano Trios* under the Opus numbers 99 and 100, had appeared, the first published by Diabelli in 1836, the other by Probst in 1828 – for which Schubert received 20 florins, 60 kreuzer – while the *Quintet* had to wait another twenty-five years, a luxury article on which a publisher made little profit.

One can see why Schubert chose a second cello for this quintet: it is used to reinforce one or other of the two pairs of instruments, and serves as their intermediary, providing an added sonority that Schubert uses most effectively, at times having an independent part, or playing in counterpoint with the other instruments, at others, joining the first cello in unison, heightening the restless, romantic atmosphere with its full, rich tone. Mozart's seven quintets with two violas showed Schubert how effective an instrument could be when used in this way, and the value of orchestral colouring added to chamber music.

The first movement, an Allegro which makes striking and skillful use of the instrumental resources, is followed by an Adagio in E major, reminiscent of *Death and the Maiden.*

This time, the development is of utter simplicity: Schubert's grandeur of inspiration, his depths of feeling are such that he has no need of recourse to technical subtleties. The instruments play often in unison, there are many repeats; only one interlude of agitation occurs to trouble the atmosphere of sweetness and divine serenity, and the intangible sadness that suffuses the whole. We admire Schubert for daring to conceive a work that owes so little to academic considerations, so much to the gift of lyrical beauty, and that is comparable with the greatest musical works of all time. The Scherzo has a fully realised orchestral texture: hunting calls, folk songs pass in the rich fabric of sound, conspiring together in a tempestuous mobility. And then with the Trio, there follows one of Schubert's most electrifying contrasts:

instead of a Presto in C major, there is an Andante sostenuto in D flat major in a different rhythm, strange music, 'languorous and funereal' said Gérard de Nerval, with the instruments used in their darker registers, in as striking contrast with the liveliness of the Scherzo as a memento mori in the hour of happiness, so that the re-statement of the Scherzo takes on a new anguish not present in the exposition.

Returning to the original mood, the Allegretto finale is all buoyancy again, and there are fresh surprises in store. We were expecting a different sort of ending, but whether Schubert was seeking to express a natural joyousness he had not known since 1823, or whether he hoped to placate the dark powers by making belief he was a carefree, happy composer, or whether, out of diffidence, he decided to give this extraordinary work an ordinary ending, he brings it to its conclusion in the popular, unpretentious idiom of the Viennese taverns, as if, after a long retirement into the depths of his soul, having laid bare its secrets, he wanted to leave us with the impression of his everyday self, as though the sufferings, longings and heavenly visions of his solitary hours had given place to the ordinary, everyday man.

(Moritz von Schwind.)

(Moritz von Schwind.)

The Church Music

In his masses, motets and other religious works, is it Schubert's spiritual self who speaks, or his Doppelgänger? One is tempted at first to answer: the inner self. He was so innately pious that he found fitting terms in which to express his faith – though it is not his religious works that seem to communicate his ultimate message.

His masses survive as decorative works intended for performance in the colourful exuberance of richly ornamented baroque churches. There is no attempt to compromise between devotion and performance, as in Beethoven's *Missa Solemnis*, Bach's Passions, Handel's Oratorios. Schubert's church works are short, naïvely affecting, ingenuous rather than solemn, of charm rather than grandeur. Nearer in style to some of Haydn's masses, they belong to the late baroque period, the Viennese countryside, and to Offices unhampered by liturgical restrictions of the Church in countries untouched by the Reformation. Thus, all Schubert's masses contain an incomplete Credo, a feature that debars them from being sung in any catholic churches except in Austria. Schubert always omits '*Et in unam sanctam catholicam apostolicam ecclesiam...*'

There are attractive passages in his second *Mass in G major*

The Stadtkonvikt. Vienna.

(2–7 March 1815), for soprano, tenor, bass and four-part choir, string orchestra and organ. The Kyrie breathes joy rather than misgiving, the Benedictus and Agnus Dei, with soprano solo, were written for Theresa Grob, and must have been a loving task. They contain melodies that are both touching and urbane, the testimony of human love to divine love. Schubert's early sense of church music is shown in the passages for the solo voices on their own, or as a trio in ensemble with the choir. He had not forgotten the lessons of Holzer, his first master: their presence is felt as an echo of the long hours spent by the boy in studying and at the Lichtenthal organ.

In his *Mass in A flat major* (1819–1822), contemporaneous with the *Unfinished Symphony*, we find introduced into Schubert's church music the more personal and lyrical mood which was to become so characteristic of him. In design, this Mass gives an impression of spaciousness, poise and tranquil beauty, though the dramatic tension of the Gloria reminds us that Schubert was at the height of his theatrical fervour, and passion breaks forth in the Credo. Choir with orchestra reiterates before each phrase the word *credo* with a decreasing intensity, until *Et incarnatus est* is reduced to choir alone, pianissimo, an impressive effect of the strong and joyful affirmation of the quickening of faith before the mystery of mysteries – contrasts that occur throughout the work, giving it its special character.

It is perhaps not in Schubert's masses that there is to be found the most direct expression of his religious feeling, but in the occasional church works, *Kyrie*, *Tantum Ergo*, offertories, and above all, in the *Salve Regina* of which he made six versions between 1814 and 1824.

The *Salve Regina* of 1815, in effect an aria from a mystical opera, composed for Theresa Grob when young Franz had not yet lost hope of love, charms us by its freshness and youthful assertiveness. The version of 1824, however, has more beauty, grandeur and simplicity, and expresses with moving conviction the hope of salvation. Meanwhile, Schubert excelled himself, not in the *German Mass* of 1827, but in the admirable *Mass in E flat* of summer 1828.

In this Mass, his longest and greatest in the full sense of the word great, the composer realised what he had hitherto only attempted: the integration of the styles of secular lyrical writing and church music. With this intention, Schubert approached his last mass as he would have a free musical work. The six ritual sections of the office are treated as Kyrie, Andante; Gloria, Allegro; Credo, Moderato; Sanctus, Adagio; Benedictus, Andante; Agnus Dei, Andante con moto, and are contrasted with one another like the movements of a symphony, in a continuous pattern of sound.

By means of the repetitions and contrapuntal development of *Cum Spiritu Sancto*, the Gloria is made to balance the Credo in length and weight; and the untroubled piety of the Benedictus is a foil to the rhythmical impetus of the Sanctus. Similarly, the forlorn and sombre opening of the *Agnus Dei*, with its reminiscence of *Doppelgänger*, is offset by the melodic beauty and quiet strength of *Dona nobis pacem*.

Though the work reaches its climax of grandeur in the impassioned urgency of the Sanctus, with its frequent modulations, striking choral entries and pulsating, almost jerky rhythms, it is the *Et incarnatus est* that reaches Schubert's lyrical heights, recalling, in its intensity, the hope of salvation so implicit in the *Salve Regina* of 1824. But this time the scale of the work, the solemnity of the Mass, add grandeur to his avowal of faith.

Angels adoring, by C. D. Friedrich.

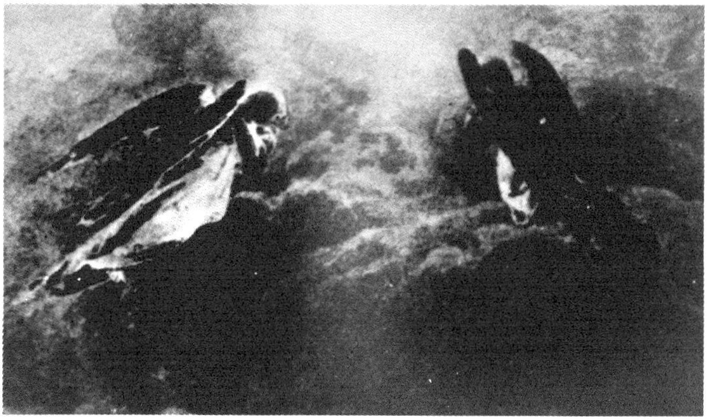

(Moritz von Schwind.)

The Symphonies

When he had found his personal expression so immediately in the lied, it still took Schubert as a symphonist a good deal of time and trouble to free himself from the influence of his first loves, Haydn and Mozart; excellent models though they were, there was a risk of Schubert's becoming restricted to an outdated style. The baroque composers were preoccupied with the society they had to entertain, aiming at elegance and wit, music that gave pleasure. It was when they wrote only to please themselves, and in some of their great works, that they truly expressed themselves – and any such stricture was not acceptable to a romantic composer.

Schubert's first three symphonies, composed in 1813 and 1815, seem to be on an equal level and to form a sequence, resembling one another in their classical manner, their animation, conciseness and their light and sparkling character. Already apparent in them is a remarkable degree of chromatic development and progressive harmony. Unlike most early work, their quick movements are more convincing and show greater invention than the andantes and adagios – an indication that although Schubert was full of the fire of youth, he had not yet reached emotional and spiritual maturity. We may

Haydn, after Guttenbrunn.

find examples in the rather foursquare Minuet of the *First Symphony*, with its Trio in Ländler style and the finale, Allegro, infectiously impudent and energetic, the sparkling treatment of the folk theme of the finale of the *Second Symphony*, the *Third Symphony's* Minuet, whose syncopations are set off by the countrified atmosphere, and this symphony's concluding rondo, a Presto Vivace of utter exhilaration. Schubert was to outgrow this careless rapture, these high-spirited frolics; luckily for us, the youth of this sixteen-year-old composer is enshrined in these early works.

The *Fourth Symphony* reveals new ambitions. Schubert had recently discovered Beethoven; he aimed at nothing less than another *Eroica*. He called his own symphony the *Tragic*. It shows an increase in growth, greater individuality, a marked preoccupation with form and unity; but one feels that Franz in 1816 had not yet either the knowledge or spiritual maturity sufficient for his purpose. His was hastily assimilated Beethoven, keenly emulated, with inadequate grasp.

Nonetheless, Schubert had the wisdom to return to his first loves in his *Fifth Symphony*, the work that is regarded as the masterpiece of his early period. In it, the spirit of the first three is brought to perfection: his premature incursion into Beethoven had not been in vain. From it he learnt to distinguish more clearly between classical and romantic, and in the light of his new knowledge, to express himself more fully in the classical style. He now knew his capabilities in a manner he wished to outgrow, which he was already outgrowing. In his *Fifth Symphony* he bids farewell to the masters of his youth. It has been said of this crucial work that it was Schubert's 'Haffner': it is the completion of a style, and the herald of another.

The *Sixth Symphony* initiates the series of labours punctuated by set-backs and fresh starts, that culminated in the *C Major Symphony* of 1828. The milestones in this process are two symphonies in the same key of C major, known as the '*Little*' and the '*Great*' – less for their actual dimensions than because of the distinction that marks Schubert's final mastery of orchestral writing in the second of the two, his last symphony. The *Sixth*, the '*Little*' *C major*, like the *Fourth*, has its inadequacies; in spite of Schubert's efforts towards a more comprehensive, sustained method of expression, his imitation of Beethoven's methods, he is still far from his model. He pays tribute to him in the Scherzo, a movement reminiscent of the Scherzo of Beethoven's *Seventh Symphony.* The Finale, with its opening march, suggests – surprisingly – Rossini. In order to formulate his style, Schubert ranges among widely differing composers. They have all something to offer him.

The *Seventh Symphony in E major* exists in sketch only, and was written in 1821, a fragment showing beauty and promise unrealised: he abandoned it without a rough draft of the score.

In the following year, 1822, he was to leave mid-way his *Symphony No. 8 in B minor,* the *Unfinished.* In April 1823, he received the honorary diploma of the Musikverein of Styria, one of the few official recognitions awarded him in his lifetime. As a mark of his appreciation, he promised in a letter of 20 September of that year to send the score of one of his symphonies.

Which one he sent is not known. At all events, he certainly sent a manuscript to Hüttenbrenner at Graz. Hüttenbrenner, instead of handing it over to the Musical Society, kept it in his desk until 1860, when he revealed its existence to the conductor Johann Herbeck, who was a great admirer of Schubert. It was incomplete.

Title page of Schubert's MS. of the Unfinished Symphony.

Since 1825, Viennese taste had undergone a change. The last of classicism had given place to romanticism, and Herbeck thought highly of the work, fragmentary as it was. Moreover, its very strangeness and mystery, the fact that it was impossible to place it with relation to Schubert's symphonic works, contributed to its success, and on 30 April 1865, Vienna acclaimed the work that was to become world-famous, and from thenceforth known as the *Unfinished Symphony*.

Hanslick has described delightedly the joy of the Viennese at their discovery of the Schubert they already loved and apprehended without as yet knowing him, and who was restored to them immortalised: 'When, after the introductory bars, the oboe and clarinet give out their suave tune in unison over the quiet murmur of the violins, any child could have recognised the authorship, and a stifled exclamation, almost a whisper, ran through the hall: Schubert! Before he has scarcely entered, they know him by his step, by the way he lifts the latch.'

Walter Dahms, basing his judgment on Beethoven's Piano Sonatas Op. 54, 78, 90, maintains that the symphony is complete, that 'if Schubert did not continue it, it is because he had nothing more to say' – an opinion we should do well to review in the light of the nine surviving bars of the Scherzo.

Obviously, Schubert left a number of unfinished compositions, among them several piano sonatas, and the famous *Quartet Movement in C minor*. So long as he did not find that he had mastered his purpose, he stopped, and left things uncompleted. His aim would seem to have been the incorporation of the inner world of the imagination within the symphonic pattern, and as a landscape is transformed in a painter's vision, he aimed to transmute traditional usage into the realm of free, lyrical contemplation – an epitome of the romantic creed of emotion and spontaneous creativity.

He aims above all at wholeness, at integrated emotion and poignancy. The two movements of the *Unfinished Symphony* do not differ substantially from one another: the initial Allegro moderato resembles in content and treatment the Andante that follows. Similarly, the instruments. He does not bother about being startling, or trying to dazzle us, but enchants us, holding us bewitched within the magic spell. The poem goes on its way, now serene, now anguished, always in Schubert's own fashion, its dynamic contrasts the tokens of emotional ebb and flow rather than simply devices in the music to vary and sustain interest. So let the sweet spell unfold, the tempests rage; we are led imperceptibly, with the end of the Andante, to a state of ecstasy. How to keep it, persuade it to remain with us? How, we wonder, could it have been possible to sustain the enchantment through two more movements? Schubert gave it up. His perfect realisation of his aim was to come six years later, with the *Ninth Symphony*.

Even so, as he left it, the *Unfinished*, which defies symphonic orthodoxy in both form and content, occupies a unique place among nineteenth century symphonies, and indeed, in the whole corpus of Schubert's works: the true inspiration of an artist still seeking to find himself. In it we see a link between Mozart's *G minor Symphony* and the *Fourth Symphony* of Brahms, the forerunner of *Tristan* and Mahler's *Song of the Earth*.

The lost symphony known as the *Gmünden-Gastein Symphony* suffered an unknown fate; no one knows what of Schubert's purpose was realised in it. Between 1822 and 1828 he composed much chamber and piano music in pursuance of his ambition to bring within the romantic orbit the classical developments of Beethoven – it is worth noting that he himself always adopted four-movement form, in traditional sequence. His last symphony does not continue the idiom of the *Unfinished*, it seems, rather, the full realisation of his fourth and sixth symphonies. The work's lay-out, its contrasted movements, in which a joyful, almost sensuous scherzo follows a dreamy, pastoral andante with a distant horn call that emanates, as Schumann has said, from another world, the tonal and rythmical treatment, brusque or subtle, all derive from a new vision. This time Schubert aspires to meet Beethoven on the plane of the *Choral Symphony*. He was successful; the tradition was to be continued by Brahms, and brought to its peak by Bruckner and Mahler. We do not know whether Schubert had heard Beethoven's *Ninth Symphony*, or whether he had simply read the score, but he obviously knew of it and knew its magnitude, and it is evident that he planned his work on Beethoven's huge scale. It was in connection with this last symphony that Schumann made his remark about Schubert's 'heavenly protractednesses' that has become famous and has often been applied mistakenly to Schubert, considering that Schumann understood 'protractedness' as duration, and by heavenly, literally the spirit of the work.

This symphony's dual character, classical and romantic, is apparent from the beginning. After a slow introduction, a grave, almost mystical statement by unison horns, a spell in which we are initiated into the primeval forests of Germanic romanticism, the Allegro's abrupt entry with its two themes of orthodox development is classical again, though with characteristics in the free and adventurous writing that are decidedly unclassical. Schubert makes full use of all his resources, bringing them all within his plan: he has never shown greater freedom, a finer invention.

Classical form, romantic spirit are happily joined in this last symphony. It was a work near to Schubert's heart, and he must have been pained at its rejection by the Society of the Friends of Music, who declined the honour of its first performance, less because of its scale than on account of its difficulty. Schubert's creative invention at its most moving is manifest in this wealth of lyric melody, in the whole organisation of this work, which, rather than a dramatic exploit, a Beethoven conflict, is a limitless pilgrimage, a journey without end, a profound yearning which bears us with Schubert into a dimension of pure music, in which all has been transmuted by his sheer poetical power. Grillparzer was disproved: it is impossible to believe that any man who could write such a work should have shown when he died, no more than great promise.

Schubert and French Romanticism

It was for his songs, and for a considerable time for his songs only, that Schubert was admired in France. In time, his piano music was performed, finally, his symphonies; though even today, none except the *Unfinished* is in the French orchestral repertory. Paul Lang in the *Revue Musicale* of December 1928, on the occasion of the centenary of Schubert's death, expressed himself on the subject of public ignorance and apathy concerning his symphonies – the last two of them of a stature comparable with the finest of Beethoven; and in 1957 he returned to the attack in his castigation of Sunday concerts which continue to offer only the *Unfinished Symphony*, – a deficiency fortunately remedied by a wide choice of recordings.

Thanks to Nourrit, who sang Schubert's songs, and Liszt who transcribed them, it did not take France generations to honour Schubert as the master of the lied. And though Liszt's piano transcriptions may appear heretical to us, they helped to make known Schubert's name and music.

In an article in the *Gazette Musicale* of 15 January 1837, Ernest Legouvé writes of the first Paris performance of Schubert's works. In the autumn of 1834, Liszt was seated at the piano at the house of a banker friend, when Nourrit entered.

Pauline Duchambge, by Lefèvre.
Top: Illustration to a romantic ballad by Pauline Duchambge.

As luck would have it, Liszt played *Erlkönig*. In the words of Nourrit's biographer Quicherat, 'As the music made its effect, Nourrit was deeply moved, and his face lit up. At the end of the piece he begged Liszt to play it again. Liszt told him that he ought to sing it, but Nourrit excused himself on the grounds that he did not know German. Liszt then explained the poem to him, and Nourrit agreed to sing the song, and sang it with inspired understanding. From that time on he became a great lover of Schubert's songs, some of them were translated at his request, and he was their untiring advocate.'

At about this time, the French vogue for romantic balladry, which began with Moncrif towards the middle of the eighteenth century, reached its height. An article in the *Gazette Musicale* of 1845 mentions the annual expenditure on these songs ... 500 fr. for one, up to 6,000 fr. for a collection of six by a fashionable composer. There was a plethora of lyric albums, musical keepsakes, ladies' offerings, etc.... Berlioz, disgusted by these compositions, poked fun at them without

Frontispiece by Dévéria to Henri Herz's 'Musical Entertainment'

effect on public taste, which found them no less exquisite. But who, today, sings the 'romances' of Paer, Bruguière, Pauline Duchambge, Amédée de Beauplan, whom Musset held to be the most characteristic of the ballad composers, and their undisputed queen, Loïsa Puget?

'The Young Persons' Keepsake' of 1835, 'a miscellany of literature, music and art' contained four novelettes, four ballads and four waltzes, one of them by Schubert, the unknown composer who was to conquer French balladry, rival it, and establish the lied in its place.

It was at the Society of the Conservatoire's first concert of the season, on 18 January 1835, that Nourrit sang *Die Junge Nonne*, and although it was placed between the *Credo* of Beethoven's *Missa Solemnis* and the *Eroica Symphony*, it did not suffer from their propinquity, but scored a tremendous success, so much so that Nourrit included it in his concert programmes at Marseilles, Lyons, Anvers and elsewhere, and others of Schubert's lieder, *Erlkönig*, which he sang at Lyons accompanied by Liszt, *Bei dir Allein*, *Ave Maria*, and *Die Sterne*. It is possible that George Sand and Musset could have been at the concert on January 18: two artists as avid for love as they were for poetry and music. At any rate, Schubert was to become one of their favourite composers.

Legouvé was not exaggerating when he wrote in his 'Recollections': 'On that day, 18 January 1835, Schubert passed in Paris from distinction to fame.'

He was already known, and known by musicians, certainly by Wartel, Dessauer, Urhan and all Liszt's circle of friends. But it was Nourrit who made him known to the general public. He did more: when he left the Opera, he would not sing at concerts except on condition that he sang Schubert. He was a wonderfully apt interpreter of these bittersweet songs of tender pathos, grandeur and tragedy. On 20 or 21 December 1834, he had already sung *Ave Maria* at Loïsa Puget's salon – it was like bringing the wolf into the sheepfold.

Among his intimate friends, and if the gathering had the right atmosphere, Nourrit would then sing *Abschied*, *Geheimnis*, *Des Mädchens Klage*, and particularly, *Gretchen am Spinnrade*. Of the latter, Ferdinand Denis wrote in his journal of 13 December 1836:

'I went to spend the evening with Chopin. This time the little party was held because George Sand wanted to meet

Adolphe Nourrit (anonymous).

Custine and, I think, Eugène Sue. She was captivating in her Turkish costume, and smokes, to my idea, to distraction... Nourrit sang *Gretchen* with less impressive conviction than when he sang it at M. de Lamennais'. But he was still extremely fine...

The death of this devotee of Schubert's was to be as sad as the composer's: he committed suicide at Naples in 1839. The funeral was at Marseilles. Chopin, who was on his way back from Majorca with George Sand, played *Die Sterne* at the Elevation of the Host, its striking sweetness and emotional fervour fitting to the occasion. 'He performed it', writes George Sand, 'not with Nourrit's glory and exaltation, but in a gentle and plaintive mood, like overtones of another world.'

Thus, ten years after his death, Schubert, unknown there in his lifetime, was renowned in the progressive circles of literary and artistic Paris. Musset says in his poem *Never*, 1839:

> Never, you said, while all the time around us
> Sounded reverberating, Schubert's plaintive notes . . .

Gérard de Nerval in *Loreley* describes his visit with Liszt to Weimar in 1850. At Schiller's, 'Liszt's fingers strayed across the yellow keys of the piano or spinet, whose pathetic inadequacy seems ludicrous when one thinks of the grand piano of today; and seeking out its depths of tone, he drew from it tender, vibrant chords that impelled one to listen with emotion to *Des Mädchens Klage*, the captivating stanzas that Schubert fitted to such a heartrending melody, and that Liszt has arranged for the piano's own characteristic tone-colour. And as I listened, I thought that the shade of Schiller should be glad, on hearing the verses that sprang from his heart, that they had found such a true counterpart in the two spirits who imparted to them an added radiance.'

George Sand, who from her childhood had had a passionate love of music, must have known Schubert's music: Liszt and Chopin must have played her his piano works before ever they were generally known to French audiences.

In her 'Intimate Journal' of 12 June 1837, when Liszt and the Comtesse d'Agoult were visiting her at Nohant, she writes: 'One evening as Franz was playing some of Schubert's most imaginative songs, the princess (Marie d'Agoult) was strolling on the terrace in the shadows . . . in a pale green dress. The moon was setting behind the great limes . . . Deep silence reigned, the breeze had dropped, expiring exhausted upon the long grasses at the first strains of the sublime instrument. The nightingale vied with it, continuing his contest, but now with a subdued, enraptured song. Like the excellent musician he is, he had drawn near in the leafy shadows, and pitched his ecstatic note in tune and time.

'We were all sitting on the steps, listening enthralled to the phrases of *Erlkönig*, now seductive, now melancholy. Lulled

George Sand and La Comtesse d'Agoult,
by Mme. Ed. Odier de la Borde.

like all nature in drowsy bliss, we could not shift our gaze from the mesmeric circle described before us by the mysterious enchantress in the white cloak. Gradually she slowed her pace as the player came to a passage of strangely sad modulations upon the tender melody.

'Then she matched her pace between the andante and the maestoso, all her movements of such grace and harmony that it seemed as if the sounds emanated from her, as if she were a human lyre. . . . At length, she sank upon a swaying branch, which yielded beneath her weight no more than if it had borne a spirit. Then the music ceased, as if, by some mysterious force, the sounds were identified with the life of this beautiful, pale woman, who seemed about to take wing toward the sphere of eternal harmony.'

It might have been a scene from *The Tales of Hoffmann*. and the lady mesmerised under the music's spell, dissolving, and assuming flesh and blood again only at the moment when the sounds ceased, the personification of the romantic muse.

It may perhaps have been in memory of this magic evening that Mme. d'Agoult composed – 'while Nourrit was singing', Liszt tells us in his 'Third Letter from a Bachelor', 11 Feb. 1838 – a paraphrase of *Erlkönig*, a type of meditation on a composer's work which, according to that charming dilettante

Caricature of Liszt by George Sand.
(André Meyer Coll.)

Jules Janin, was to become very popular. 'With an unusual reversal, it is no longer the composer who makes music to the poet's words, but the poet who writes words to the composer's music – George Sand intoned a magnificent hymn on the song *The Highwayman*, on hearing a rondo fantastique by Liszt. Musicians and poets alike applauded this poetical rendering of a kind that was quite new to us.' Janin also devotes several pages to Schubert in his 'Winter Symphonies' of 1858.

Alas, Schubert is not mentioned in *La Comédie Humaine* by Balzac, who, in the midst of the craze for Rossini, developed a passion for Beethoven – one that was cured in 1834, doubtless under the influence of Mme. Hanska. One remembers his modest pronunciation: 'Beethoven is the only being capable of arousing my jealousy. I should like to have been Beethoven more than Rossini or Mozart. There is a divine power in the man.' But Balzac discounted the most poetical composer of all time, and there is the same omission in the works of Stendhal, Mérimée and Baudelaire, for whom Weber was the personification of musical romanticism:

> Where, under a mourning sky, mysterious fanfares
> Pass, like a muted echo of Weber.

Meanwhile, the Complete Works of Schubert had appeared in 1837 – a title that was a naïve claim, as the collection comprised only some sixty lieder out of six hundred. Bélanger made the translations, Sorrieu supplied the illustrations. Two years later followed a new edition under the imprint of Schlesinger, this time with adaptations by Emile Deschamps and lithographs by Devéria. Legouvé comments: 'The romance has been killed by the lied. See, in *Die Junge Nonne* by Schubert, *The Trout*, *Auf dem Wasser zu Singen*, how basically the accompaniment is integrated with the melody, how completely at one it is with it! Try, then, when you are sated with this sustaining, noble music, reverting to the burblings of Loïsa Puget.'

Apart from Berlioz, who had such scant recognition in France during his lifetime, were there only such musicians as Loïsa Puget, Pauline Duchambge? The music of French romanticism was certainly not the equal of its literature and art.

Notwithstanding, Léon Guichard, in his detailed and intelligent study *Music and Letters of the Romantic Period* (Presses Universitaires de France, 1955), does not take too harsh a view. 'Besides the triumphs of bel canto, the useless feats of virtuosity' he remarks, 'there is real enthusiasm, and for a worthwhile object. In the intimate circles of like minds revolving around Liszt and Chopin, there is the cult of Mozart, Beethoven and Schubert, which communicates the love and traditions of great art. We picture in imagination Stendhal at *The Green Huntsman* listening to Mozart, Nerval listening to old songs in the forest of Ermenonville, Berlioz fascinated by Liszt's Bach playing, George Sand crouching by Liszt's beautiful piano, Chopin playing *Die Sterne* at Nourrit's funeral. For these faithful souls, the romantic period in France deserved perpetuation.'

AVE MARIA

Mélodie

de François Schubert.

transcrite pour le Piano

par

F. LISZT.

Prop. des Edit^rs

Prix : 4^f 50^c

A PARIS, chez RICHAULT, Editeur, Boulevart Poissonnière, N° 16, au Premier.

ROMANCE

D'Anna Lyle.

Musique de F. Schubert

Paroles françaises de M. D. P.

dédiée

à M.lle FALCON.

Artiste de l'Académie Royale de Musique!

Par l'Auteur des Paroles.

Propriété de S. Richault Prix 2f 50c

The Poverello of Romanticism

History has not yet allotted to Schubert his final place: he is still a much-discussed composer, unequalled as a song-writer, of debatable merit as a symphonist and sonata writer. The little schoolmaster, son of a domestic, humble, self-deprecating *Schwammerl* . . . these legendary images mask the face of the artist who is the real Schubert.

In his lifetime, as since, he was eclipsed by the titanic Beethoven, the Byronic, tempestuous Weber. In the company of the immortals, he is looked on as the poor little father of the romantics, whose genius is hailed with the qualification of 'Yes – oh yes, but . . .'

To the majority of people who indulge in facile classification and who make arbitrary distinction as to rank and achievement, Schubert may be neatly tucked into the middle group near the tail end of the top half. First come the great three, Bach, Mozart, Beethoven; next – it may be – Wagner, Brahms, Debussy; in the third rank, Schubert, Schumann, Chopin, Ravel.

However this may be, appraisement in such hierarchical terms is useless. Each artist makes his own unique contribution with no terms of reference other than his own. Those practically necessary words 'great' and 'little' become meaningless when

Schubert's room in the Wipplingerstrasse. (Drawing by Moritz von Schwind, 1821.)

applied to the emotions or the creations of the mind – a 'great love', yes: but who ever heard of a small one? For love all metaphors are inadequate. So, with a composer: the expression a 'great' one has become a commonplace, though to designate any as small would be totally contrary to the canons of art and truth, since music is an absolute, defying definition, as Schubert defies classification.

In Romanticism he should take his place not as the poor author of its being, but as its Poverello – its Little Poor One. For like his patron saint Franciscus Seraphicus, Francis of Assisi, he was lowly, bearing his greatness in secret.

Because of his plainness, his diffidence, his humble birth and lack of social status, he has come to be regarded as a sort of *Cousin Pons*. Attractive enough to be loved by women, ambitious enough to receive the freedom of fashionable circles, sagacious and volatile as a prince of bohemians, he was nevertheless ill served by his mild goodness and unconcern in a world of whose rank and distinctions he remained oblivious. If he had indulged in recrimination towards God and man, or had given way to despairing of humanity, he would have been proclaimed a bad artist, his poverty laid at the door of the State's neglect of its creative citizens, his death ascribed to want of proper care. As it was, it was his own guileless, sweet nature that attracted to itself the faithful love and friendship that were his consolation for the success he never knew.

In the course of the nineteenth century the portrait of him that we know and love was filled out by his family and friends. In it, we see him, the innocent child of nature, happily in the clouds, scarcely descending from them even at times of too much wine, too little food. Music poured from him as though his genius was merely its filter, it took possession of him as a medium is possessed by a spirit. He was a dreamer, to whom his life, the world and himself were all part of the dream. He did not seek to leave the imprint of his personality upon his surroundings, or to make his mark on his time: he lacked the dynamic drive, the will to power, preferring to empty himself so that he might the better serve his vision of music, be no more than his Emperor's humble subject, to be most wholly himself in the realm of his art. He must have conceived of the happy life as one that would fulfil his own special dream of the love and goodness, the sensibility, joy of nature, affections and simple pleasures that were of the substance of his music. He was a contemplative – not of the energy and activity of Theresa of Avila, but untroubled, unworrying, indifferent to both struggle and triumph. He preferred to take everything on trust, and would have liked fortune and the fame he unambitiously desired, to have come to him fortuitously – as if genius were ever rewarded by the world that ignores it! More than that is necessary: success must be willed to be won, and once won, must be maintained. Schubert never appreciated what he had won in open conflict on his own merits; it lacked the element of the fabulous essential to his nature. Might not what happened in the fairy tales also happen in real life? and Beauty realise the suffering soul of the Beast and fall in love with that which had seemed unlovable, the ragged slut be the Prince's dream-beloved.

Schubert knew and felt his uncomeliness; trusting in providence, he hoped that Beauty would pity him and love him, that he would be changed into Prince Charming in the mind and heart of the one he loved. In his eyes, love bereft of magic, without its enigma, was not worthy the name.

Schubert knew he was of no importance, like Jean-Paul's intriguing character Maria Wuz, a bohemian, an inconsiderable schoolmaster; but he hoped that he would find sympathy in the civilised minds of his time, and that they would apprehend the spirit beneath its cloak, for he knew that he had an unique contribution to make – one that came from the full heart of a wistful child. He reckoned without the public's indifference, the envy of some, the easygoing triviality of others who were only too ready to leave him to the obscurity in which he lived contentedly and troubled no one. If his music was performed on occasion at the insistence of his friends, no one bothered their heads about this harmless dreamer. If Schubert had had the notion to 'arrive', what opposition he would have encountered!

The failure of his theatrical venture was a matter of satisfaction to his rivals. When he died, not a single Vienna newspaper carried a notice of his funeral – he vanished as unobtrusively as he had lived.

Certainly Schubert's music is an enigma, with a significance far beyond the Zeitgeist, the spirit of his age, in the period and circumstances of Metternich's bid to check the Revolution by the Holy Alliance, in the victorious Vienna of the 1820's. It is bittersweet music, sad, grave, at times tragic, in contrast with the heedless, peacefully-ordered life of its composer. His character, with his yearning for affection, his sociability and easy-going nature, would lead one to expect pleasing, light, unexacting music of typically Viennese charm; instead of which he offers us a restless, passionate creation, awakening our secret longings, our grief for our lost paradise; its least definable factor, unconjecturable from his age and circumstances, being its supernatural quality which, being God's, has also been called the devil's.

How is it, then, that a composer of such classical foundations can merit the title of the first of the Romantics? In actual fact, he did not devise a new musical language, was not an innovator, an inventor of form or usage, the exploiter of a system. He adhered to the conventions, the anatomy of classical form, so permeating them with poetic beauty that in the *Unfinished Symphony* or the *Piano Sonata in A minor Op. 42*, we are confronted with works that are a very different proposition from a Haydn Symphony or a Mozart Sonata. He gave himself body and soul to his lifelong project, realised in his last years, of the lyrical integration of the lied within larger forms in the classical tradition. Thus, endowed with melodic and harmonic gifts greater even than Beethoven's, he remains in all his work, both chamber and orchestral, essentially a lyrical composer. We can only imagine how formidably he would have rivalled for all time the

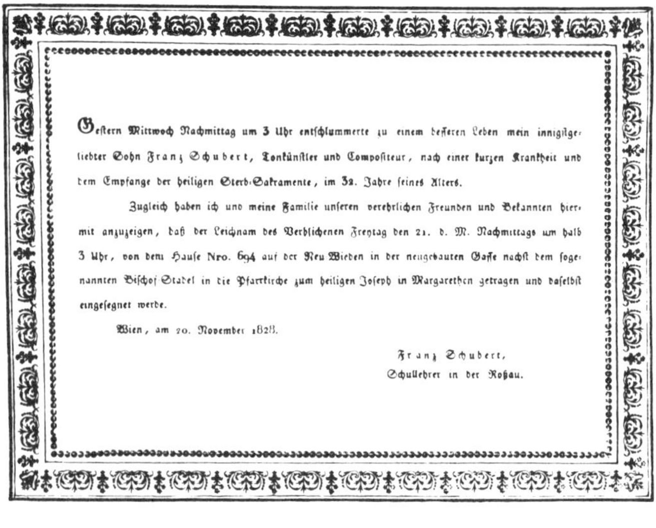

Gestern Mittwoch Nachmittag um 3 Uhr entschlummerte zu einem besseren Leben mein innigstgeliebter Sohn Franz Schubert, Tonkünstler und Compositeur, nach einer kurzen Krankheit und dem Empfange der heiligen Sterb-Sakramente, im 32. Jahre seines Alters.

Zugleich haben ich und meine Familie unseren verehrlichen Freunden und Bekannten hiermit anzuzeigen, daß der Leichnam des Verblichenen Freytag den 21. d. M. Nachmittags um halb 3 Uhr, von dem Hause Nro. 694 auf der Neu-Wieden in der neugebauten Gasse nächst dem sogenannten Bischof-Stadel in die Pfarrkirche zum heiligen Joseph in Margarethen getragen und daselbst eingesegnet werde.

Wien, am 20. November 1828.

Franz Schubert,
Schullehrer in der Roßau.

Announcement of Schubert's death.

Schubert in Heaven.
Design by Otto Böhler for the Schubert Centenary. →

composers of the nineteenth century, if he had lived fifteen or twenty years longer and realised fully the final mastery he was achieving – though it is hard to imagine that he would ever have written more moving works. He said what was in him to say in his own fashion, as we who listen today hear it, stirred, enthralled, transported.

For if his attainment does not embrace the inception of new form or utterance, his own unique contribution to music lies in his approach to the inner music of the imagination, its transformation at his hands, as he raised it to new heights, new significance, in works that are creations of the absolute, the mirror of the emotions, the image of another world – an achievement, at his death, of genius not unfulfilled.

Chronology

	SCHUBERT	THE OTHERS
1784	Schubert's father leaves Moravia for Lichtenthal, Vienna.	Beaumarchais' *The Marriage of Figaro.*
1785	17 Jan. marries Elisabeth Vitz.	
1786	Appointed master of the Lichtenthal school and settles at 'The Red Crayfish', birthplace of Schubert.	Mozart's *The Marriage of Figaro.*
1791		29 Feb. Rossini born. 5 Dec. Mozart dies.
1792		November: Beethoven comes to Vienna and studies with Haydn.
1796		*Wilhelm Meister's Apprenticeship:* Goethe.
1797	31 January: Schubert born	Treaty of Campo-Formio between France and Austria. *First Symphony* of Beethoven. *Hyperion* by Hölderlin. Tieck's *Tales.*
1798		*The Creation:* Haydn.
1799		*Spiritual Canticles:* Novalis.
1802		*Die Jungfrau von Orleans:* Schiller. *Génie du Christianisme:* Chateaubriand.
1803		11 December: Berlioz born.
1804		18 May: Bonaparte becomes Napoleon I. George Sand born.
1805		14–15 November: Vienna occupied by the French. Napoleon at Schoenbrunn. 2 December: Austerlitz. Schiller's *William Tell.* Schiller dies. *Fifth Symphony* of Beethoven.
1807		Insurrection against Napoleon at Madrid.
1808	October: Schubert enters the Convict; angelic chorister at the Royal Chapel.	1806–1808: *Des Knabens Wunderhorn:* Arnim and Brentano.

Battle of Austerlitz (F. David.)

	SCHUBERT	THE OTHERS
1809		3 Feb. Mendelssohn born. 31 May: Haydn dies. 6 June: Wagram.
1810	Schubert's earliest known composition: Fantasy in G for Piano Duet.	8 June: Schumann born. Musset born.
1812	First *String Quartet*.	Sack of Moscow. Chopin born. *Seventh Symphony* of Beethoven.
1813	Schubert leaves the Convict end of October. Enters the Normal School for a year's course. 28 Oct: *First Symphony*.	1812–1813: Retreat from Russia. 22 May: Wagner born. 10 October: Verdi born.
1814	Autumn: assistant in his father's school. *First Mass in F major*. 19 Oct: *Gretchen am Spinnrade*. Falls in love with Theresa Grob.	Congress of Vienna. *Fidelio* by Beethoven.
1815	Autumn: *Erlkönig*. Tries in vain for appointment at Laibach.	18 June: Waterloo.

Engraving for Erlkönig.

	SCHUBERT	THE OTHERS
1816	*Fourth* and *Fifth Symphonies.*	25 April: Byron leaves England. *The Barber of Seville:* Rossini. *Elixiere des Teufels:* Hoffmann.
1817	Obtains a year's leave. Leaves his father's house. May-Aug: *Piano Sonatas.*	Feb: Byron finishes *Manfred.*
1818	Feb: *Sixth Symphony.* Sept.-Nov: Visits the Esterhazy family at Zelesz in Hungary.	
1819	Autumn: *The Trout Quintet.*	
1820	19 Aug: *The Magic Harp.*	*Premières Méditations:* Lamartine.
1821	*Gesang der Geister über den Wassern.*	*Freischütz:* Weber.
1822	Feb: *Alfonso and Estrella.* Sept.: *Mass in A flat major. Unfinished Symphony* begun. *Wanderer Fantasy.*	16 August: Shelley's funeral pyre near Viareggio. Feb: Byron finishes *Don Juan.* E.T.A. Hoffmann dies.
1823	April: *The Domestic Campaign.* May-Nov: *Die Schöne Müllerin.* Falls ill.	*La Barque de Dante:* Delacroix. Rossini settles in Paris. *Ninth Symphony:* Beethoven.
1824	Summer: second visit to Zelesz. Caroline. *Octet. String Quartet No.* 13 in F minor.	19 April: Byron dies.
1825	*Gastein Symphony.* Aug: *Die Junge Nonne.* Visits the Tyrol with Vogl.	Jean-Paul Richter dies. Weber dies. *A Midsummer Night's Dream:* Mendelssohn.

Engraving for The Wanderer.

	SCHUBERT	THE OTHERS
1826	*Death and the Maiden Quartet.* (begun Mar. 1824) *String Quartet No.* 15 *in* G major.	*Odes and Ballads:* Victor Hugo.
1827	*Winterreise.* 2 *Piano Trios.* 8 *Impromptus.* *Fantasy* for Violin and Piano.	26 March: Beethoven dies. *Faust* translated by Gérard de Nerval. Heine's *Poems.* *Peter Schlemihl:* Chamisso.
1828	*Symphony No.* 9 *in C maj.* *Fantasy in F minor* for Piano, four hands. *String Quintet in C major.* *Schwanengesang.* 3 *Piano Sonatas* Op. posth. 19 November: Schubert dies.	16 April: Goya dies at Bordeaux.
1829		10 April: Berlioz sends Goethe the score of *Eight Scenes from Faust.*
1835		18 Jan: Nourrit sings *Die Junge Nonne* in Paris.
1840		Chopin plays *Die Sterne* at Nourrit's funeral.
1865	17 Dec.: First performance of the *Unfinished Symphony*, Vienna.	

Engraving for Die Schöne Müllerin.

't by Mälher

Bibliography

A brief selection only is given from an extensive list. For bibliographies see particularly Deutsch, Dahms, Friedlaender, Gérold, Grove, Gumprecht, Heuberger, Hutchings, Kobald, Kreissle, von Hellborn, Niggli, Reissmann and Wurzbach.

The standard edition of Schubert's works was published by Breitkopf and Härtel, Leipzig, 1884–1897, 40 vols.

DEUTSCH, OTTO ERICH : Schubert. *A Documentary Biography*. Translated by Eric Blom. London, 1947.
in collaboration with D. R. Wakeling: *Schubert, Thematic Catalogue of his works in Chronological order*. N.Y., 1950.

BLOM, ERIC : *Schubert. Novello's Biographies of Great Musicians*. Pp. 14. London, 1938.

EINSTEIN, ALBERT : *Schubert, a Musical Portrait*. N.Y., 1951.

FLOWER, NEWMAN : *Franz Schubert, the Man and his Circle*. rev. ed. London, 1949.

HUTCHINGS, ARTHUR : *Schubert. The Master Musicians*. London, 1945.

BROWN, MAURICE J. E. : *Schubert, A Critical Biography*. London, 1958.

Joseph Teltscher, self-portrait.

Schubert's Principal Works

For numbering see the thematic catalogue by Otto Deutsch.

VOCAL MUSIC

a) Lieder

Listed under the authorship of the poem (total number 603).

CLAUDIUS, *Der Tod und das Mädchen.*

CRAIGHER, *Die Junge Nonne.*

GOETHE, *Gretchen am Spinnrade.*
Schäfers Klagelied.
Scene aus Goethes Faust.
Rastlose Liebe.
Erlkönig.
Jägers Abendlied.
Ganymed.
Prometheus.
Heidenröslein.
Meeresstille.
Wanderers Nachtlied.
Der Fischer.
Erster Verlust.
Suleika I & II.
Der Musensohn.
Am Flusse.
An Schwager Kronos.
Über allen Gipfeln.

HEINE, Six poems from *Heimkehr*, Nos. 7–13 of *Der Schwanengesang.*

MATTHISSON, *Die Schatten.*
Lebenslied.

(Waldmüller.)

MAYRHOFER, *Auf der Donau.*
Einsamkeit.
Abendstern.

RELLSTAB, *Ständchen.*

RUCKERT, *Du bist die Ruh.*
Sei mir gegrüsst.

SCHILLER, *Des Mädchens Klage.*
Der Jüngling am Bache
Sehnsucht.
Der Taucher.
An Emma.
Hoffnung.
Die Götter Griechenlands.

SCHLEGEL, *Lob der Thränen.*

SCHOBER, *An die Musik.*

SCHUBART, *Die Forelle.*

b) Song Cycles

GOETHE, *Songs from Wilhelm Meister* (1826).
1. (*Duo*) *Mignon und der Harfer.*
2. *Mignon's Song: Heiss mich nicht reden*
3. *So lasst mich scheinen.*
4. *Mignon's Song: Nur wer die Sehnsucht kennt.*

MÜLLER, *Die Schöne Müllerin* (1823).
Die Winterreise (1827).

SCOTT, *Seven Songs from The Lady of the Lake* (1825).

RELLSTAB, HEINE, SEIDL, *Der Schwanengesang* (1828).

c) Various Voices

Canons for 3 voices.

Five Duos for voices or Horns.

UZ, *An die Sonne* (1816), with piano.

FOUQUÉ, *Gebet* (1824), for soprano, alto, tenor and baritone.

KLOPSTOCK, *Begräbnislied* and *Osterlied*, vocal quartet and piano.

d) Choral Works for Female Voices

GRILLPARZER, *Ständchen* (1827), for contralto, chorus and piano.

e) Choral Works for Male Voices

GOETHE, *Gesang der Geister über den Wassern* (1821).
Sehnsucht (1819).
Im gegenwärtigen Vergangenes.

SEIDL, *Grab und Mond* (1826).
Nachthelle (1826).
Nachtgesang im Walde (1827), with 4 horns.

f) Cantatas

GRILLPARZER, *Miriams Siegesgesang* (1828).
NIEMEYER, *Lazarus oder Die Feier der Auferstehung* (1820) unfinished.

CHURCH MUSIC

Kyrie (3) chorus; *Tantum ergo*, chorus (1828); (Op. 45), chorus, (1822); *Salve Regina*, chorus (1816); (Op. 153), soprano (1824); tenor, (1814).
Offertories: (Op. 46), soprano and tenor; (Op. 47), soprano, tenor and chorus (1828); *Tres sunt*, chorus. *Stabat Mater*, chorus (1816); (Klopstock), solo voices and chorus (1816).

Mass in F major (1814).

Mass in G major (1815).

Mass in B flat major (1815).

Mass in C major (1816).

Mass in A flat major (1822).

Mass in E flat major (1828).

German Mass in F major (1827).

Psalm XXIII (1820).

Psalm XCII (1828).

CHAMBER MUSIC

a) Duo Sonatas

VIOLIN AND PIANO
3 *Sonatinas* (1816): No. 1 in D major, no. 2 in A minor, no. 3 in G minor.
Sonata in A major (1817) Op. 162, called the *Grand Duo*.
Fantasy-Sonata in C major, (1827?) Op. 159.
Rondo brillant (1826) Op. 70.

VIOLONCELLO AND PIANO
Sonata in A minor (1824), '*arpeggione*'.

FLUTE AND PIANO
Introduction and Variations on Trock'ne Blumen (1824), Op. 160.

b) String Trios

B flat major, one movement (1816).
B flat major, four movements (1817).

c) Piano Trios

B flat ('*Sonata*' one movement, 1812) Op. 99.
E flat major (1827), Op. 100. Op. posth. 148.

d) String Quartets

No. 1, *B flat major* (1812).

No. 2, *C major* (1812).

No. 3, *B flat major* (1813).

No. 4, *C major* (1813).

No. 5, *B flat major* (1813).

No. 6, *D major* (1813).

No. 7, *D major* (1814?).

No. 8, *B flat major* (1814), Op 168.

No. 9, *G minor* (1815).

No. 10, *E flat major* (c. 1817), Op. 125, No. 1.

No. 11, *E major* (1816), Op. 125, No. 2.

No. 12, *C minor* (Quartet Movement) (1820).

No. 13, *A minor* (1824) Op. 29, No. 1.

No. 14, *D minor* (Death and the Maiden) (1826).

No. 15, *G major* (1826) Op. 161.

e) Piano Quartet

Adagio and Rondo concertante (1816), for piano, violin, viola and cello.

f) Quintets

Rondo in A major for violin and string quartet (1816).

A major ('the Trout') (1819), Op. 114, for piano, violin, viola, cello and double bass.

C major (1828), Op. 163, for 2 violins, viola and 2 cellos.

g) Miscellaneous

Quartet for guitar, flute, viola and cello (1814?).

Octet, F major (1824), Op. 166, for 2 violins, viola, cello, double bass, clarinet, bassoon and horn.

PIANO MUSIC

Two Hands

a) Variations

Ten Variations on an original theme (1815).

Thirteen Variations on a theme by Hüttenbrenner (1817).

Variations on a Theme by Diabelli (1821).

b) Dances

Minuets, Ecossaises, Allemandes, Ländler, Waltzes, inc. *Valses nobles* Op. 77, and *Valses sentimentales* Op. 150. *Marches, Gräzer Galopp*, 2 *Scherzos* (1817).

c) Sets

Six Moments Musicaux (1824–1827) Op. 94.

4 *Impromptus* (1827) Op. 90.

4 *Impromptus* (1827) Op. 142.

3 *Klavierstücke* (1828).

d) Fantasies

Fantasy (*Wanderer*) (1822) Op. 15.

Fantasy Sonata No. 18 *in G major* (1826).

e) Sonatas

21 *Sonatas*, inc.

No. 10 *in A major* (1819) Op. 120.

No. 16 *in A minor* (1825) Op. 42.

No. 19 *in C minor* (1828) Op. posth.

No. 20 *in C major* (1828) Op. posth.

No. 21 *in B flat major* (1828) Op. posth

Four Hands

Overtures, 10 *Polonaises* (c. 1825) Op. 61 and 75, *Marches*, *Variations*, inc.

Variations on a French Song (1818) Op. 10: *Fantaisies*, inc. *Fantasy in F minor* (1828) Op. 103; *Rondos*, *Divertissement à la hongroise* (1824) Op. 54;

Sonatas, incl. *Grand Duo*, C major (1824) Op. 140.

WORKS FOR THE STAGE

See p. 69-71

ORCHESTRAL WORKS

SYMPHONY *No.* 1, *D major*, (1813).

No. 2, *B flat major* (1815).

No. 3, *D major* (1815).

No. 4, *C minor* ('*Tragic*') (1816).

No. 5, *B flat major* (1816).

No. 6, *C major* (The 'Little' C major) (1818).

No. 7, *E major* (sketch) (1821).

No. 8, *B minor* ('*Unfinished*') (1822).

No. 9, *C major* (*the 'Great' C major*) (1828).

Overtures, *Dances*.

A selected discography from Great Britain

CHAMBER MUSIC

- *Sonata for Violin and Piano in A major (Op. 162)*
  Johanna Martzy (violin) and Jean Antonietti (piano) Columbia 33CX 1399
- *Piano Trio No. 1 in B flat major (Op. 99)*
  Schneider, Casals and Istomin Philips ABR 4059
- *Piano Trio No. 2 in E flat major (Op. 100)*
  Schneider, Casals and Horszowski Philips ABL 3009
- *Piano Quintet in A major ("The Trout")*
  Wührer (piano) and the Barchet Quartet. Vox PL 8970
- *String Quartet No. 2 in C major (Mozart: Quartet No. 17)*
  Italian Quartet Columbia 33CX 1367
- *String Quartet No. 8 in B flat major*
  Italian Quartet Decca LXT 2855
- *String Quartet No. 10 in E flat major (Op. 125 No. 1)*
  Amadeus Quartet HMV ALP 1337
- *String Quartet No. 13 in A minor (Op. 29)*
  Budapest Quartet Philips ABR 4069
- *String Quartet No. 14 in D minor ("Death and the Maiden")*
  Koeckert Quartet Deutsche Grammophon DGM 18043
- *String Quartet No. 15 in G major (Op. 161)*
  Budapest Quartet Philips ABL 3158
- *Quartet for Guitar, Flute, Viola and Cello*
  Birkelund, Neumann, Erikson and Friisholm Decca LXT 5070
- *String Quintet in C major (Op. 163)*
  Stern, Schneider, Katims, Casals and Tortelier. Philips ABL 3100

– *Octet for Strings and Wind in F major (Op. 166)*
Vienna Octet Decca LXT 2983

ORCHESTRAL MUSIC

Rosamunde: Incidental Music (Op. 26)
Vienna State Opera Orchestra conducted by Dean Dixon.
Westminster WLP 5182

Symphony No. 1 in D major
Symphony No. 2 in B flat major
Royal Philharmonic Orchestra conducted by Sir Thomas Beecham
Philips ABL 3001

Symphony No. 3 in D major
Symphony No. 4 in C minor ("The Tragic")
Berlin Philharmonic Orchestra conducted by Igor Markevitch.
Deutsche Grammophon DGM 18221

Symphony No. 5 in B flat major
Symphony No. 8 in B minor
Vienna Philharmonic Orchestra conducted by Karl Böhm
Decca LXT 5381

Symphony No. 6 in C major
London Symphony Orchestra conducted by Josef Krips
Decca LXT 2585

Symphony No. 8 in B minor ("The Unfinished")
Concertgebouw Orchestra conducted by Eugen Jochum
Philips ABR 4021

Symphony No. 9 in C major ("The Great")
Berlin Philharmonic Orchestra conducted by Furtwängler
Deutsche Grammophon DGM 18347
New York Philharmonic Orchestra conducted by Bruno Walter
Philips ABL 3074

PIANO MUSIC

FRIEDRICH WUHRER

Sonata No. 3 in E major
Sonata No. 11 in F minor Vox PL 9800

Sonata No. 4 in A minor
Sonata No. 20 in A major (Op. Post.) Vox PL 9130

Sonata No. 9 in B major
Sonata No. 19 in C minor (Op. Post.) Vox PL 8420

FRIEDRICH WUHRER

Sonata No. 13 in A major (Op. 120)
Sonata No. 18 in G major (Op. 78) Vox PL 8590

Sonata No. 14 in A minor
Sonata No. 21 in B flat major (Op. Post.) Vox PL 8210

Sonata No. 16 in A minor (Op. 42)
Wilhelm Kempff Decca LXT 2834

Grand Duo for four hands in C major (Op. 140)
Paul Badura-Skoda and Joerg Demus. Westminster WLP 5093

Eight Impromptus (Op. 90/142)
(Sonate No. 13)
Paul Badura-Skoda Westminster WLP 6205

Six Moments Musicaux (Op. 94)
(Wanderer)
Adrian Aeschenbacher Deutsche Gramophon DGM 19001

Fantasia in C major ("Wanderer").
Clifford Curzon Decca LX 3059

SONG CYCLES

Die Schöne Müllerin (Op. 25)
Dietrich Fischer-Dieskau (baritone) and Gerald Moore (piano)
HMV ALP 1036-7

Die Winterreise
Dietrich Fischer-Dieskau (baritone) and Gerald Moore (piano)
HMV ALP 1298-9

Schwanengesang
Hans Hotter (baritone) and Gerald Moore (piano)
Columbia 33CX 1269

CHORAL MUSIC

Mass in A flat major
Soloists, Choir and the Vienna Pro Music Orchestra conducted by Ferdinand Grossmann Vox PL 9760

Mass in E flat major
Soloists, Akademie Kammerchor and the Vienna Symphony Orchestra conducted by Rudolf Moralt Vox PL 7840

A selected discography from America

CHAMBER MUSIC

Sonata for Violin and Piano in A major (Op. 162)
Fritz Kreisler (violin) and Rachmaninoff (piano) Victor LVT 1009

Piano Trio No. 1 in B flat major (Op. 99)
Fournier, Janigro and Badura-Skoda Westminster 18481

Piano Trio No. 2 in E flat major (Op. 100)
Busch-Serkin Trio Columbia ML 4654

Piano Quintet in A major ("The Trout")
Amsterdam Quintet Epic 3LC 3046

String Quartets (complete)
Vienna Konzerthaus Quartet Westminster 18472-9

String Quartet No. 13 in A major (Op. 29)
Fine Arts Quartet Mercury 10065

String Quartet No. 14 in D minor ("Death and the Maiden")
Budapest Quartet Columbia ML 4832

String Quartet No. 15 in G major (Op. 161)
Budapest Quartet Columbia ML 4833

String Quintet in C major (Op. 163)
Weiss, and the Vienna Konzerthaus Quartet Westminster 18265

Octet for Strings and Wind in F major (Op. 166)
Vienna Octet London LL 1049

ORCHESTRAL MUSIC

Rosamunde: Incidental Music (Op. 26)
Concertgebouw Orchestra conducted by Eduard Van Beinum
London LL 622

Symphony No. 1 in D major
Symphony No. 2 in B flat major

Royal Philharmonic Orchestra conducted by Sir Thomas Beecham
Columbia ML 4903

Symphony No. 3 in D major

Cincinatti Symphony Orchestra conducted by Thor Johnson
London LL 405

Symphony No. 4 in C minor ("The Tragic")

Concertgebouw Orchestra conducted by Eduard Van Beinum
London LL 736

Symphony No. 5 in B flat major

Vienna Philharmonic Orchestra conducted by Karl Böhm
London LL 1105

Symphony No. 6 in C major

Colonne Association Orchestra conducted by Georges Sebastian
Urania 7137

Symphony No. 7 in E major (Orchestration Weingartner)

Vienna State Opera Orchestra conducted by Franz Litschauer
Vanguard 427

Symphony No. 8 in B minor ("The Unfinished")

Philadelphia Symphony Orchestra conducted by Bruno Walter
Columbia ML 4880

Symphony No. 9 in C major ("The Great")

NBC Symphony Orchestra conducted by Arturo Toscanini
Victor LM 1835

PIANO MUSIC

Sonata No. 9 in B flat major (Op. 147)
Sonata No. 19 in C minor (Op. Post.)

Friedrich Wührer Vox 8420

Sonata No. 13 in A major (Op. 120)

Badura-Skoda Westminster 18154

Sonata No. 16 in A minor (Op. 42)

Wilhelm Kempff London LL 792

Sonata No. 18 in G major (Op. 78)

Jolles Haydn Society 81

Sonata No. 21 in B flat major (Op. Post.)

Wilhelm Kempff London LL 307

Grand Duo for four hands in C major (Op. 140)

Paul Badura-Skoda and Joerg Demus Westminster WLP 5093

Eight Impromptus (Op. 90/142)

Artur Schnabel Victor LTV 1019

Six Moments Musicaux (Op. 94)

Edwin Fischer HMV 1055

Fantasia in C major ("Wanderer")

Istvan Nadas Period 719

SONG CYCLES

Die Schöne Müllerin (Op. 25)

Inez Matthews (Mezzo) and Franz Holletschek (piano) Period 713-4

Die Winterreise

Hans Hotter (baritone) and Gerald Moore (piano) Angel 3521-3

Schwanengesang

Monteneau Westminster 18692

CHORAL MUSIC

Mass in A flat major

Soloists, Choir and the Vienna Pro Musica Orchestra conducted by Ferdinand Grossmann Vox 9760

Mass in E flat major

Soloists, Akademie Kammerchor and the Vienna Symphony Orchestra conducted by Rudolf Moralt Vox PL 7840

ICONOGRAPHY

Photos Anderson-Giraudon: pp. 6-7.

Photos Bulloz: pp. 150, 154, 170.

Club des Librairies de France: pp. 2, 81.

Photos Roger-Viollet: pp. 31.

Photos W. Speiser, Basle: pp. 9, 10, 22, 24-25, 26a, 27, 29, 35, 37, 43, 50, 51, 52, 56-57, 59a, 62-63, 68-69, 75, 88, 89, 93, 99, 113, 126, 137, 138, 145 162, 167, 172, 173, 174.

End paper: 'View of the Prater, Vienna', engraving by C. Postl after Janscha.

DATE

APR 18 '82

APR 17 '86

JUN 26 '86

GAYLORD